What People Are Saying

"A new and brilliant understanding of how to unleash the latent capacity within you, the church and every group for the Jesus mission. *Activating 5Q* gives us both a framework and a practical application from Ephesians 4 for how to activate the Body of Christ. This needs to be read by every leader who loves the church, its people and its mission."

DAVE FERGUSON,
lead pastor of Community Christian Church; lead visionary for
NewThing; author of *Finding Your Way Back To God* and *Starting Over*

"I believe that there are few topics more important for the renewal of Christ's people and the subsequent transforming of the world around us than what is addressed here."

NEIL COLE,
author of *Organic Church*, *Primal Fire*, and *One Thing*

"Inspires, provokes and engages. It will be a catalyst for mission in the years to come!"

DANIELLE STRICKLAND,
international social justice advocate; author and speaker

5Q

ALAN HIRSCH & JESSIE CRUICKSHANK

ACTIVATING 5Q
A USER'S GUIDE

MOVEMENTS

First published in 2018 by 100M
100movements.com

ISBN 978-0-9986393-2-1

Typeset in Sabon MT Std & Brandon Grotesque by
Palimpsest Book Production Ltd, Falkirk, Stirlingshire

Printed in Colombia

Cover design by Ben Connolly

APEST summary sheet © Kevin Miller, used with permission

For all the believers on mission, who endeavor to live in the way of Jesus and seek to build the Kingdom with one another in his image. We are his people, his church.

My Foursquare family, specifically Tammy Dunahoo and Sam Rockwell, for giving me the best job in the world.

My husband, who is God's great gift of love to me.

—Jessie

I would like to dedicate this book to all my sisters in the Lord who so deeply enrich our world. I can't imagine a world without women. You are so often overlooked, but I want to say that "I see you" and am so very grateful. I will always honor and serve you.

Special thanks to those women who have contributed directly to the writing of this book—the brilliant Jessica Cruickshank, the queenly Anna Robinson, the always-inspirational Danielle Strickland, and my beloved partner in everything, Deb Hirsch.

—Alan

Contents

Dear Reader

Our world is volatile, changing at a faster pace than ever. We live in uncertain times. The church has lost the voice and authority that Christendom, for good or ill, afforded us. Yet many of us are still on catch up, operating as if Christendom is alive and kicking. The maps we have inherited from our Christendom past no longer fit the territories of our post-Christendom present; it's like we are trying to negotiate New York City using a map of Los Angeles! We tweak our practices in the hope that maybe, just maybe, it will be enough. But tinkering a little here and there will never truly bring the systemic change that is so desperately required.

What we really need is a new map, a new paradigm . . . a new frame of reference to help us see, think, and live differently. We need to lay down our churchly habits and be willing to pick up *a new pair of glasses.*

We believe 5Q provides us with a new lens, a new paradigm. It's nothing new or flashy, but rather a return to what Jesus has already put in the Body of Christ to help us fulfill the Great Commission. We believe that it will take *all five* of the gifts of Jesus to the church—the apostolic, the prophetic, the evangelistic, the shepherding, and the teaching capacities—operating together in their fullness in the Body of Christ, to carry out our mandate. We need the APEST to fulfill the Great Commission and command of Jesus.

5Q simply allows the Body of Christ to see and reactivate what Christ has already given us through the fivefold ministry.

We know that changing the map is, in some ways, simple. But it's also incredibly hard. It requires *change*. Change in our own hearts and minds. And it requires *courage*. Courage to live into a new reality and push beyond the status quo.

Our hope is that this book will challenge you to live into a new way of seeing, thinking, and living. But we also hope that this book and the associated tests will equip you, your organization or church to take concrete steps toward living that out.

We are truly excited about the journey you're about to take. We pray that this book will guide you into an ever-greater fullness of truth in Christ Jesus and for courage and power to apply the insights gained along the way.

Come and join us on the 5Q adventure that awaits!

This Book . . .

- will be used most effectively in teams;

- is meant to be scribbled on, discussed and used out in the real world. Take it off the shelf and put it into practice;

- is written for small group leaders, missional community leaders, house church leaders, parents, volunteers and congregational leaders;

- will help you to reflect on your learning, with questions at various points to assist you in that process. We recommend taking the time and space to absorb the information and reflect on what it means for you and your team in your particular context;

- simplifies and explains the core themes of 5Q, equips you with some 5Q tools, and explores the journey of 5Q growth and maturity. For a more comprehensive theological and cultural exploration of 5Q, we recommend reading the associated book, *5Q: Reactivating the Original Intelligence and Capacity of the Body of Christ* (available to buy at www.5qcentral.com), as well as *The Permanent Revolution* and *Playbook*.[1]

What's Inside?

There are three sections to this book:

Section One: Explain (*The Foundations*)

This section provides some key definitions, looks at the purposes of APEST for the church, covers the core themes of 5Q and explains why we propose APEST as valid marks of the church. If you've read the accompanying book, this will refresh your knowledge. There are reflection questions interspersed throughout to help you process and apply the information in your own context.

Section Two: Equip (*The Tools and Tactics*)

This is where the rubber hits the road! This section helps you as an individual and an organization to grow in 5Q by providing accessible tools and tactics to help you develop and mature 5Q in your context.

Section Three: Explore (*The Journey*)

This short section prepares you for the journey ahead with an explanation of what 5Q growth and maturity will look like, as well as providing information for further resources and coaching.

There is also an appendix at the back of the book which provides an important accompaniment to the two 5Q tests (the 5Q Diagnostic and the 5Q Systems Analysis) which help to evaluate your organization's current expression of the fivefold.

'STOP' Points

Throughout the book there are key points to STOP.

We are making an assumption that if you're reading this book, you want to grow as a disciple. As disciples, we are essentially learning to hear and obey Jesus.

The STOP boxes provide opportunities to reflect on your learning (**Awareness**) and consider how you will apply what you have learnt (**Application**).

These STOP boxes will contain various key questions, examples of which are given below:

STOP

Awareness

Understanding Questions e.g. What have you learnt?
Paradigm Questions e.g. How does this change the way you see and think?
Realizations e.g. Where do you already see this at work or see this afresh?

Application

Behavior/Practice Questions e.g. How will you put this into practice personally, in your team and context?

Synergy Questions e.g. How can you release potential and see greater fruitfulness and greater maturity through service, unity, learning or partnership?

SECTION ONE

EXPLAIN
(THE FOUNDATIONS)

Introduction

Beginning at the Beginning

You might be an APEST veteran, or you might be completely new to the conversation. Whatever your starting point, we want to start by outlining some of the key concepts, which will help build toward an understanding of 5Q. You might want to keep coming back to some of these concepts, so mark the page.

Defining APEST

Below is an overview of the fivefold functions as outlined in Ephesians 4:1–16.

- The *apostle/apostolic*:
  "Sending and extending"
  In Greek, the term apostle literally means "sent one." As the name itself suggests, it is the quintessentially missional (from *missio*, the Latin equivalent) ministry. The French translation of the term apostle (envoy) picks up this sense of commission much better than the English transliteration—an apostle is an envoy. It is a pioneering function of the

church, the capacity to extend Christianity as a healthy, integrated, innovative, repro-ducing movement, ever-expanding into new cultures. It also takes care and responsibility for the ongoing integrity of the core ideas (DNA, organizational principles, or meta-ideas) that generate and maintain systemic health across the organization.

- The *prophet/prophetic*
  "Questioning and embodying"
  The prophetic is the function tasked with maintaining loyalty and faithfulness to God above all. Essentially, prophets are guardians of the covenant relationship that God has with his people. The prophetic is also passionately concerned with living a life morally consistent with the covenant—a simple and authentic life of justice, holiness, and righteousness. The prophet proclaims God's holiness and calls for holiness in God's people (1 Peter 1:16).

- The *evangelist/evangelistic*
  "Recruiting and connecting"
  The evangelistic function involves the proclamation of the good news at the core of the church's message. Evangelism is therefore all about the core message and its reception in the hearts of people and cultures. The evangelist is the storyteller, the all-important recruiter to the cause, the naturally infectious person who is able to enlist people into what God is doing in and through the church.

- The *shepherd/shepherding*
  "Developing and deepening relationships"
  Shepherding is the function and calling responsible for maintaining and developing healthy community and enriching relationships. This involves a commitment to nurture spiritual maturity, maintain communal health, defend the community against breakdown, and engender loving community among the redeemed family of God.

- The *teacher/teaching*
  "Training and contextualizing"
  The teaching function is concerned with the passing on of wisdom and understanding. This involves bringing a comprehensive understanding of the revelation given to the church. It is a guiding and discerning function. A biblical understanding of this function emphasizes wisdom, not simply speculative philosophy. Teaching, of course, also involves integrating the intellectual and spiritual treasure of the community and encoding it, in order to pass it on to others and to the next generations.[2]

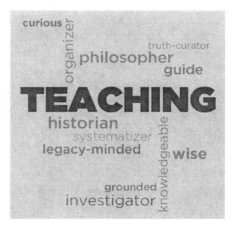

© Kevin Miller

Functions and Callings—What's the Difference?

One key thing to note at this stage is that 5Q largely focuses on *functions* rather than *callings*, so it's important to appreciate the difference. If you know anything about APEST, you have probably considered it primarily through the lens of your own and others' callings. "I'm an apostle," you might say, "and my associate is a pastor." As understanding of APEST has grown within the church, much of the focus has been on these individual *callings*, rather than on the APEST *functions*. We wholeheartedly believe that each disciple should seek to understand and live into his or her own individual calling. (You can do a personal profile at www.5qcentral.com/tests.) But over the last few years we have begun to appreciate the significance of the APEST capacities *coming together* in an organization, and what those *functions* look like when operating in symphony.

CAPACITIES	OBJECTIVES
PRACTICES	DUTIES
ESSENTIALS	EXTENSIONS
INSTINCTS	AGENCIES
PURPOSES	GENERATIONS
SENSES	MISSIONS
ROLES	ACTIONS
CATEGORIES	SERVICES
FUNCTIONS	DIMENSIONS
IDENTITIES	TYPES

Synonyms of Functions

And so the focus of this book, as well as the accompanying tests, is primarily on the *functional* aspect of APEST; this will begin to make more sense as the book unfolds.

To illustrate the difference, consider functions and callings in a business organization:

> Any business will have distinct *departments* such as product design and development, marketing, human resources, each responsible for particular *functions* necessary for the whole organization to thrive. (Functions)

Each department will have *individuals* who will fulfill the roles particular to the department function. For instance, the marketing department is the right context for the role of a marketing manager; the job of Chief Financial Officer is filled by an appropriately suited accountant. **(Callings)**

Bringing it back to APEST: when the various fivefold capacities are expressed in an **individual**, we term that *calling*. When these capacities are expressed by a **group of people** in an organization, we call them *functions*.

Take a look at the table below to compare the difference between *functions* and *callings* for each of the APEST:

	Function	Calling
Apostolic/Apostle	seed/guard core ideas DNA, maintaining sentness, translocal networking, pioneering, church planting	missional leaders, church planters, pioneers, organizational designers, networkers, innovators
Prophetic/Prophet	maintain covenant relation with God and others, holy discontent, prayer, justice	social activists, artists, incarnational missionaries, holy dissenters, worship leaders
Evangelistic/Evangelist	cultivate attractive culture, broadcast vision, storytelling, open recruitment process	recruiters, storytellers, communicators, apologists, entrepreneurs
Shepherding/Shepherd	cultivate community, inclusiveness, family culture, social glue, develop organizational EQ	community workers, healers, protectors, spiritual directors, caregivers
Teaching/Teacher	foster learning, educational processes, tools & resources, theologizing, understanding	teachers, philosophers, theologians, guides, coaches, educators, researchers

Table 1.1 APEST Functions and Callings

STOP

Awareness

Do you know what your personal APEST calling is?
(If not, try taking the optional but recommended APEST profile test at:
www.5qcentral.com/tests)

Summarize the difference between functions and callings.

Which parts of the role you currently have in church ministry matches your APEST calling and which parts don't?

Do you, or does your church or organization, value some functions more than others? If so, why do you think this might be the case?

Application

What steps could you take to ensure your role more accurately reflects your APEST call?

What changes could you make to help those you lead to operate in a role that reflects their APEST call?

How can you model and demonstrate equal worth of each of the fivefold?

Defining 5Q

We're going to unpack 5Q as we go along. But here's something to get you started.

First, let's think about Emotional Intelligence (EQ) to help us understand Fivefold Intelligence (5Q). We can define Emotional Intelligence as the ability to:

Recognize and *understand* our own emotions and the emotions of others (Awareness)

and

Manage our own emotions and *influence* the emotions of others.[3] (Application)

Emotional Intelligence is therefore a combination of **awareness** and **application**. In order to have a high EQ, it's not simply enough to be **aware** of our own and other people's emotions. We need to **apply** that knowledge to manage our own emotions and influence others in order to achieve desirable outcomes.

Now let's apply this to 5Q.

5Q is the ability to:

Recognize and *understand* APEST in the broadest and deepest way possible, in God, creation, culture and the Body of Christ (Awareness)

and

Live out and *release* the fullness and maturity of the ministry of Jesus in our own and in other people's lives. (Application)

In order to have high 5Q, it's not simply enough to recognize and understand the full extent and capacities of APEST. Our knowledge and understanding must be activated and applied symphonically to bring about maturity and fullness, particularly in the Body of Christ.

NOTES

Key Headlines to Reflect On

Key Discussion Topics to Process

Key Action Points for Next Steps

1

The Purposes of APEST for the Body of Christ

Hopefully as you've read the definitions of APEST and of 5Q you can already begin to appreciate the value of APEST. But let's take a look at the key APEST text in Ephesians 4 to help us understand the *purposes* of APEST for the Body of Christ. Before we dig a little more into Ephesians 4, it's important to note that the whole book of Ephesians is generally considered to represent best thinking about the church. It can be viewed as a spiritual template for the church, shaping the thinking and behaviour of the Body of Christ throughout the centuries.

There are three natural sections within the overall unity of verses 1–16, so let's consider how they relate to APEST:

1. Unity of the Church (Ephesians 4:1–6)

As a prisoner for the Lord, then, I urge you to live a life worthy of the calling you have received. Be completely humble and gentle; be patient, bearing with one another in love. Make every effort to keep the unity of the Spirit through the bond of peace. There is one body and one Spirit, just as you were called to one hope when you were called; one Lord, one faith, one baptism; one God and Father of all, who is over all and through all and in all.

The text at the beginning of Ephesians 4 flows out of Paul's famous prayer for the church in 3:14–21. Here he prays that they grow up into the fullness of Christ in the world. Immediately after, he goes on to appeal to the Ephesians (and to all Christians everywhere) to live consistently with who God is and what he has done in Jesus . . . to "live a life worthy of the calling [we] have received" (4:1).

The strong appeal of verses 1–6 is that *we are not to separate what God has put together*. We are to strive for the unity of the Spirit, knowing there is one God, one faith, one baptism, etc. And insofar that 1–6 is connected with what follows in 7–11, we are not to break APEST up either. In his ascension, Jesus has "given" APEST to the church. In other words, *the fivefold is a part of the church's inheritance in Jesus*. We are to treasure the fivefold because we treasure Jesus and what he is doing through us.

2. Jesus' Gift to the Church (Ephesians 4:7–11)

But to each one of us grace has been given as Christ apportioned it. This is why it says:

> "When he ascended on high,
> he took many captives
> and gave gifts to his people."

(What does "he ascended" mean except that he also descended to the lower, earthly regions? He who descended is the very one who ascended higher than all the heavens, in order to fill the whole universe.) So Christ himself gave the apostles, the prophets, the evangelists, the pastors [shepherds] and teachers . . .

Paul goes on to affirm the God-given nature of the ministry of the Body of Christ. He clearly states in verses 7 and 11 that Jesus "gave" APEST to the church, distributing it among all the people as he saw fit. We're going to get a little bit technical with the grammar here, but it will be helpful, so stick with us. The verb form used for "given"[4] is an aorist indicative, a resolute verb form perfectly suited for use in constitutions. Aorists reflect actions that took place in the past and are therefore once-and-for-all-time events. Aorist indicatives are historic in a similar way that the signing of the Declaration of Independence was historic—it will impact America's self-understanding for all time. The aorist indicatives used in Ephesians 4:1,7,11 demonstrate that APEST has, *once and for all*, been bequeathed to the Body of Christ. It happened; it cannot and will not be revoked. We need to feel and understand the weight of the grammar that Paul uses to talk about the constitutional *givenness* of the APEST ministries to the church.

And Paul is also trying to communicate that the APEST functions come as an *inseparable* unit. In Ephesians 4:7–11, all five APEST ministries come together under the sway of the ruling verb, *edothe* (verses 7, 11). The result is that the *one verb attaches to all* the APEST functions . . . Christ *gave* the apostles, he *gave* the prophets, he *gave* the evangelists, he *gave* the shepherds, he *gave* the teachers. *APEST comes as a unit or not at all.* Use of this verb form is the strongest way Paul can say that the fivefold functions/callings are *always* a built-in part of the Body of Christ. Because each function/calling contributes something to the Body that the others do not, they complement and enhance each other. We are not to cherry-pick one, two or three of the APEST, as we have tended to do in church history. The church should always be sending and extending (A), questioning and embodying (P), recruiting and connecting (E), developing and deepening relationships (S), and should always be training and contextualizing (T). *All* are needed in *every time* and in *every place*.

3. Maturity and Fullness in Christ (Ephesians 4:12–16)

. . . to equip his people for works of service, so that the body of Christ may be built up until we all reach unity in the faith and in the knowledge of the Son of God and become mature, attaining to the whole measure of the fullness of Christ.

Then we will no longer be infants, tossed back and forth by the waves, and blown here and there by every wind of teaching and by the cunning and craftiness of people in their deceitful scheming. Instead, speaking the truth in love, we will grow to become in every respect the mature body of him who is the head, that is, Christ. From him the whole body, joined and held together by every supporting ligament, grows and builds itself up in love, as each part does its work.

This section answers the question, "Why, in his ascension, did Christ give the fivefold to the church?" The purpose of the fivefold functions is clearly stated by Paul in the key Ephesians text itself, as follows:

i) "For the building up/completing of the Body" (v.12)

The Body of Christ is a system, much like the human body. Activating APEST is actually a way of healing and restoring the Body from its dysfunction—Paul explicitly says this in Ephesians 4:12! He uses the word *katartismós* which is normally translated as "equip." But *katartismós* can equally be translated as "mend what has been broken or rent" (as in nets and even broken bones), to "perfectly join together," "put in order," "adjust," "strengthen," "perfect or complete," and "make one what one ought to be."[5]

And so reading verse 12 through those various translations, we can say, Jesus appointed some to be apostles, prophets, evangelists, shepherds, and teachers, for . . .

- equipping
- perfecting
- mending
- perfectly joining together
- putting in order
- ethical strengthening
- completing
- fulfilling
- healing

. . . of the saints, for the work of the ministry.

All five functions are critical for the church to self-regenerate, develop, and "perfect" itself! In other words, the APEST system, as a whole, is like the self-healing capacity in your body. Your body has an inbuilt ability to self-regenerate, and so if you were wounded in an accident or ravaged by a disease, your body has the capacity to heal itself: it has an intrinsic ability to be restored to functionality.

This body analogy is also perfectly true for the *Body* of Christ! All five functions are needed so that the Body of Christ might be perfected, healed, restored, and that it might self-generate, grow, and develop. It offers us a newfound wholeness to our identity, functionality, and ministry. On the other hand, if we exclude APEST from the equation, we will exclude our capacity to be made whole and function as Jesus intended us to in the first place.

ii) "That we might reach the fullness of Christ" (v.13)

This is an incredible statement! Paul says that there is a *direct relationship* between APEST and the church's capacity to "attain to . . . the fullness [Gk. *pleroma*] of Christ." Surely this ought to cause us to sit up and pay attention! The central purpose in Christian discipleship is for each one of us to *become more like Jesus* and to allow Jesus to *live his life in and through us*. What Paul is saying here is APEST brings the capacity for the Body of Christ to collectively live into the fullness of Christ so that Christ might fill everything in every way (Ephesians 1:22–23). Without APEST, the church's capacity to attain to the fullness of Christ is at stake. *In other words; no APEST, no fullness.*

iii) "For the maturing of believers in community" (vv.12–13)

Paul says that one of the main purposes of the fivefold functions is to bring about *the maturing of the church* (vv. 12–13). In other words, without APEST the church can never fully mature. The Western church has rarely been the kind of church envisioned in verses 12–16. It's hardly surprising when we consider that for years the church has only really validated the shepherd and the teacher (ST). The Western church has ignored the apostolic, prophetic and evangelistic gifts. If we've become over-attached to selective forms of ministry or organizational systems, then we can and must change, and allow Jesus to re-establish the functionality of his Body through the application of APEST.

It is important to emphasize here that maturity can only happen in *community*. There is no other way for the church to mature than as a Body of believers. We are designed for relationship, for interaction with others. We can't learn language, how to smile, how to thrive, or even how to love without the social and emotional aspect of life. Without community and loving relationships, we will fail to thrive,[6] let alone mature.

Therefore, if the Body of Christ is going to mature, it is critical that all capacities of APEST find an expression in the church or organization. The church's ability to thrive and come into the full maturity of Christ (Ephesians 4:13, 15) depends on it.

STOP

Awareness

How has what you've just read expanded your thinking on the purposes of APEST for the Body of Christ? (You can re-read the text from Ephesians on page 20.)

Reflect on how you would explain the importance of APEST to a friend or colleague.

Application

Make a note of your friends, leaders and team members and reflect on how they express their APEST calling in their context. Start with three to five people.

Prepare a three-minute summary of the key components and purpose of APEST to share with a friend or colleague.

Ephesians 4

Unity and Maturity in the Body of Christ

As a prisoner for the Lord, then, I urge you to live a life worthy of the calling you have received. [2] Be completely humble and gentle; be patient, bearing with one another in love. [3] Make every effort to keep the unity of the Spirit through the bond of peace. [4] There is one body and one Spirit, just as you were called to one hope when you were called; [5] one Lord, one faith, one baptism; [6] one God and Father of all, who is over all and through all and in all.

[7] But to each one of us grace has been given as Christ apportioned it. [8] This is why it says:

> "When he ascended on high,
> he took many captives
> and gave gifts to his people."

[9] (What does "he ascended" mean except that he also descended to the lower, earthly regions? [10] He who descended is the very one who ascended higher than all the heavens, in order to fill the whole universe.) [11] So Christ himself gave the apostles, the prophets, the evangelists, the pastors and teachers, [12] to equip his people for works of service, so that the body of Christ may be built up [13] until we all reach unity in the faith and in the knowledge of the Son of God and become mature, attaining to the whole measure of the fullness of Christ.

[14] Then we will no longer be infants, tossed back and forth by the waves, and blown here and there by every wind of teaching and by the cunning and craftiness of people in their deceitful scheming. [15] Instead, speaking the truth in love, we will grow to become in every respect the mature body of him who is the head, that is, Christ. [16] From him the whole body, joined and held together by every supporting ligament, grows and builds itself up in love, as each part does its work.

NOTES

Key Headlines to Reflect On

Key Discussion Topics to Process

Key Action Points for Next Steps

2

5Q: What's the Big Idea?

Thomas Edison is famously quoted as saying, "When you have exhausted all possibilities, remember this: you haven't." Given all my research, writing, and training on the fivefold over many years, I (Alan) thought I had pretty much exhausted APEST possibilities. Yet, the more I began to delve into it, the more I began to see that APEST actually continues to shape not just the church, but *all* human culture. And so in this chapter, we're going to do a whistle-stop tour of APEST as a system— what we have come to call 5Q.[7] Stay with us on the journey as we expand our thinking!

APEST is Laced throughout Creation

Did you know that the church didn't invent the APEST terms?

It may come as a surprise, but all the APEST words are actually derived from functions *already* existing in society. For instance, *apostle* was a secular term describing an empowered agent sent to conduct business on behalf of others, or as an ambassador of royalty. Prophets are described throughout ancient-near-Eastern culture and the Greco-Roman world. Evangelists were heralds. Shepherds were evident throughout and used as a metaphor of roles in society, and teachers are clearly present in all forms of culture. Whether people were part of the first-century church or not, they would be familiar with the different APEST roles and their function within society.

Each of these functions existed *before* Jesus and were woven by God into the fabric of creation. There have always been inventors and visionaries, prophets and "seers," messengers and marketers, protectors and caretakers, sages and philosophers.[8] APEST has therefore always shaped, and continues to shape, not just the church, but *all* human culture.

Perhaps it's easier to see this if we view APEST as a type of *cultural template* occurring throughout human personality, society and culture. The five patterns are archetypes: the recurring symbols, controlling metaphors, myths, patterns, and governing ideas that shape culture and society. Archetypes exist in many forms, but one obvious expression of archetypes is in what social scientists call the "hero-expressions" of a given group in culture. Heroes can be broadly grouped according to the fivefold categories. For instance, apostolic heroes could be seen in the forms of founders, rugged pioneers, military strategists and leaders, architects and designers of new forms, entrepreneurs and innovators. Prophetic-style heroes will likely come in the form of artists, seers, reformers, and iconoclasts. Heroes in the evangelistic mold are likely to be the culture's storytellers, those who mobilize action, and those who spread key ideas. The shepherd hero expression would include those who rigorously defend the community, elders who shape and guide it, and the humanizers who make it liveable for all. Teacher-philosopher heroes abound in all societies. These include the sage, mentor, the scientist, among others (see figure 2.1 below).

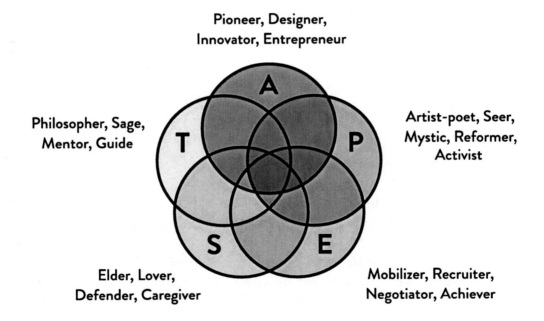

Figure 2.1 APEST Heroes Types and Roles throughout Creation

We can also view APEST through an aptitude or capacity lens. Each of the fivefold archetype or hero perceives, processes, and engages the world in very different and specific ways. Each particular function *has a unique paradigm or bias* that others do not possess and cannot see. Above all, each brings an enhanced capacity to the multidimensional tasks of any organization. Each of the fivefold can also be characterized by a type of intelligence: apostolic intelligence (AQ), prophetic intelligence (PQ), and so on. The combination of the five intelligences creates a synergistic, heightened intelligence in the people of God as a whole (see figure 2.2 below).

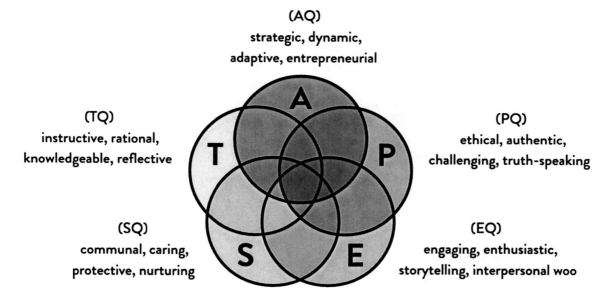

Figure 2.2 Archetypes of APEST Intelligences and Capacities throughout Creation

APEST is Active in Society and Culture

Once we start to acknowledge that APEST can be found throughout creation and expressed through individuals and organizations, we can begin to explore the possible implications for disciples in all the various domains of society. This might include the arts, recreation-entertainment, architecture-construction, politics, media, industry, economy, education, family, government, media, health, science, and religion.[9] Possibly the most obvious way to apply APEST thinking beyond the church is in the area of general leadership theory and practice.

As we have already seen, Ephesians 4 speaks directly of fivefold leadership *equipping* followers, *building* them up, and helping the *entire* Body of Christ come to *unity* and *maturity*.[10] There are numerous leadership typologies, each with their own criteria of categorization. Even though they may differ, all assume rightly that leaders usually have their own distinctive patterns of process, thought, and behaviour, which can be categorized under discrete types. For instance, we can describe entrepreneurial leaders in a way that clearly distinguishes them from other types. Similarly, we can describe less risk-engaging leaders who excel at developing and expanding existing organizational systems. Leaders have certain observable characteristics which can be categorized. After many years of reflection on leadership, organization, and practice, I (Alan) believe APEST is up there with the very best of categorizations.

APEST could be used as an excellent categorization of leadership to help in the recruiting, developing, and maximizing of leadership teams in any type of organization. In my first book, I suggested the following as a possible way of structuring leadership using APEST typologies, and suggested that this would make for an excellent, well-proportioned, team in any setting.[11]

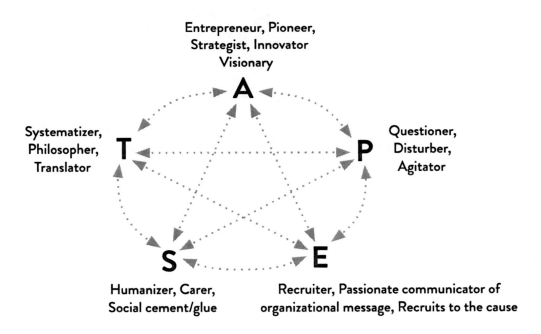

Figure 2.3 Organized for Impact

As we have already mentioned, APEST functions exist in all major sections of culture and economy. As table 2.1 below shows, there are many segments of society that express these functions and have taken on the role of maturing individuals in these capacities, through different forms of higher education, training, and leadership programs.[12]

This is exactly the creation and culture that Jesus wants to redeem. As his disciples, we are called to express Christ to our culture and generation. The Great Commission (Matthew 28:18–20) sends us to make disciples in every aspect of society. We are to be missionaries to our schools, hospitals, communities, businesses, and industries. We are to bring the Kingdom of God in *all* places, by living out and modeling the redeemed APEST capacities. This is what it means for the Body of Christ to be made manifest in the world. *All the world is not called to be found in the church; the church is called to be found in all the world.*[13]

We believe that part of the *ecclesia*'s role, in both the lives of believers and in society, is to equip people through the maturing of these gifts. What if a person learned more about how to be a good teacher from their believing community than from a secular education? This would require well-trained and wise teachers to be sharing and leading in the community of believers. What if we could learn how to be a good storyteller (evangelist) from others in our faith community? Ephesians 4 is clear that the church is commanded to be an equipping agency in all of the APEST capacities. These are provided through the natural gifts, talents, and education of the members of the Body.

We are not saying that believers should abandon secular education. Secular culture may actually be more effective in maturing some of these capacities than the church currently is. Up to now, secular education has played a greater role in maturing people in their APEST capacities because the church has generally ignored the fivefold. While the church has been focused elsewhere, society has taken up the cause of maturing people in their gifts. We believe that a high-level APEST organization can only happen within the context of a faith community, but in order for that to happen there must be a focus on developing these capacities into maturity.

The following table lays out some ways in which we can see the fivefold functions used beyond the community life of the church and in broader society.

Table 2.1 APEST in Archetype, Culture and Hero-Expression

APOSTLE

Archetypal APEST	Hero-Expression in General Culture	Categories of Intelligence	Domains of Society	Universal Examples (in life and myth)
Founder, General, Visionary, Pioneer, Adventurer (A)	Breakthrough designers, Innovator-entrepreneurs, Paradigm shifters, Cultural architects, Organizational designers, Movement-makers, Systems thinkers, Business leaders, Problem-solvers, Imagineers, Start-ups	Strategic, Dynamic, Adaptive, Entrepreneurial Other characteristics include: Strategic, Holistic, Future-oriented, Pattern-sensitive, Innovative, Adventurous, Creative, Ideational, Design-oriented	Business, Politics, Architecture, Law, Governance, Innovation and Entrepreneurship	Steve Jobs, Catherine Booth, Jim Collins, Franklin Delano Roosevelt, Joan of Arc, Theodore Herzl, Angela Merkel, William Clark and Meriwether Lewis, George Washington, Osama bin Laden, Adam Smith, Karl Marx, Thomas Edison, Vladimir Lenin, Genghis Khan, Neo (*The Matrix*), Captain Jean-Luc Picard (*Star Trek*), Aragorn (*LOTR*)

PROPHET

Archetypal APEST	Hero-Expression in General Culture	Categories of Intelligence	Domains of Society	Universal Examples (in life and myth)
Seer, Warrior, Poet, Reformer, Questioner, Meaning-Maker (P)	Artists, Poets, Shamans, Ethicists, Activists, Futurists, Liberators, Meaning-makers, Revolutionaries, Advocates, Existentialists, Anarchists, Hackers, Spiritualists, Mystics, Environmentalists, Whistle-blowers, Aid workers, Psychologists, Politicians, Feminists, Quality controllers	Ethical, Authentic, Challenging, Truth-speaking **Other characteristics include:** Artistic, Loyalist, Spiritual, Future and present-oriented, Principled, Contrarian, Intuitive, Predictive, Aesthetic, Sympathetic, Passionate, Urgent, Critical	Arts, Psychology, Politics, Aid and Development, NGOs, Environmentalism, Ethics	Bono, Simone Weil, Eleanor Roosevelt, Mahatma Gandhi, John Lennon, Friedrich Nietzsche, Emmeline Pankhurst, Nikola Tesla, Salvador Dali, Pablo Picasso, Malcolm X, Bob Dylan, Leonard Cohen, Rumi, Søren Kierkegaard, Aldous Huxley, Doctors Without Borders, Gandalf (*LOTR*), Morpheus (*The Matrix*)

EVANGELIST

Archetypal APEST	Hero-Expression in General Culture	Categories of Intelligence	Domains of Society	Universal Examples (in life and myth)
Messenger, Achiever, Believer, Guerilla Leader, Champion, Storyteller (E)	Mobilizers, Recruiters, Negotiators, Media workers, Achievers, Marketers, Organizers, Miracle-workers, Communicators, Preachers, Dealers, Raconteurs, Journalists, Motivational speakers, Networkers, Buccaneers, Sales, Public relations	Engaging, Enthusiastic, Storytelling, Interpersonal woo

Other characteristics include:

Relational, Communicative, Existential, Emotional, Genuine, Inspirational, Optimistic | Media and communication, Charismatic leadership, Business, Politics, Advertising, Marketing | Seth Godin, Malcolm Gladwell, Oprah Winfrey, Bill Clinton, Tony Blair, Katy Perry, Richard Branson, Tony Robbins, Zig Ziglar, Trinity (The Matrix), Zorro (Zorro) |

SHEPHERD

Archetypal APEST	Hero-Expression in General Culture	Categories of Intelligence	Domains of Society	Universal Examples (in life and myth)
Caregiver, Defender, Peacemaker, Helper, Servant, Selfless, Healer (S)	Elders, Lovers, Guardians, Loyalists, Humanizers, Parents, First responders, Cultivators, Mediators, Military, Counselors, Health workers, Priests, Community workers, Human resources, Police	Communal, Caring, Protective, Nurturing, Other characteristics include: Empathetic, Relational, Familial, Sociable, Seek common good, Event-oriented, Engaging, Communal, Personal, Affectional, Protective	Medicine, Family, Psychology, Community development, Police, Defense	Nelson Mandela, Colin Powell, Mother Teresa, Florence Nightingale, Dag Hammarskjöld, Aung San Suu Kyi, J.R.R. Tolkien, J. Edgar Hoover, Malala Yousafzai, Chris Kyle (*American Sniper* is based on his story)

TEACHER

Archetypal APEST	Hero-Expression in General Culture	Categories of Intelligence	Domains of Society	Universal Examples (in life and myth)
Sage, Thinker, Observer, Philosopher, Guide, Scientist (T)	Philosophers, Sages, Instructors, Ideologists, Investigators, Information workers, Scientists, Educationalists, Mentors, Thinkers, Disciplers, Theoreticians, Debaters, Engineers, Researchers, Theologians, Accountants, Forensics, Legal workers	Instructive, Rational, Knowledgeable, Reflective Other characteristics include: Philosophical, Insightful, Analytical, Forensic, Past-oriented, Interpretative, Descriptive, Meaning-oriented, Critical	Education, Science, Philosophy, History, Publishing, Engineering	Socrates, Plato, Albert Einstein, Lao Tzu, Hannah Arendt, Julian Huxley, Abraham Heschel, David Attenborough, Helen Keller, Alain de Botton, Stephen Hawking, Yoda (from the Star Wars movies)

STOP

Awareness

Consider people from your own congregation or community. Using table 2.1, identify one individual for each of the fivefold who you can observe operating in their APEST calling in their workplace or their neighborhood.

(Take a look at "APEST in the Workplace: Seeing 5Q in Everyday Spaces" on pages 94–96 of chapter five to see how you can identify 5Q personalities in a work environment.)

Does your church or organization provide opportunities and pathways for individuals to grow in their APEST gifting? If so, what are they?

Application

Who could invest and apprentice you to grow in your fivefold maturity and particular APEST calling?

Think about what steps you could take to help your ministry, church or organization to recognize and value APEST functions in the workplace or in their neighborhood.

Below is an example of how one leader has helped his congregation to do this:

> "As I teach through the gifts, we are interviewing members of the church body to ask them to discuss how that week's specific gift is lived out in their public-sector life (third place, work place, families, etc.). Letting everyday people be the heroes has been huge, as well as giving practical examples for those still learning the 5Q language."
>
> Jon Ritner, Ecclesia Hollywood

What training processes could you begin to put in place to enable others to grow in their APEST gifting? Think of two people and one next step for each of them.

APEST is Found in the Nature and Purposes of God

So if the fivefold archetypes can be seen in and throughout culture and history, it begs us to ask: *Where did these archetypes come from in the first place?* Surely they didn't just pop out of nowhere! If we agree that creation bears God's imprint as Creator, then we can logically say that the APEST archetypes are grounded in the various aspects of God, as revealed to us in the Bible:

- Aspects of God that relate to design, creation, purpose, and mission are likely the roots of the apostolic in his creation and church.
- God's holiness, his personal nature, his anger at all injustice and unrighteousness, and his covenantal love infuse what has become known as the prophetic.
- The evangelistic function draws upon those aspects of God related to his saving, redeeming, and celebratory nature.
- God's love, his desire for relationship and intimacy, likely infuse what has become known through the shepherding functions in human society and church.
- The teaching function is derived from God's wisdom, the fact that he is all-knowing, that he is the source of reason and revelation.

And so we can see that APEST comes from God himself and flows from him into creation, as summarized in table 2.2 below.

Table 2.2 God Is . . .

Function	God is . . .
APOSTLE	• the source—all things come from him • designer—he is creator and foundation of all • missional—the sent and sending God • the electing and predestining God—he works all things for good • sovereign—he is King over all creation

Function	God is . . .
PROPHET	• faithful—his word and nature are utterly true and dependable • revealer—God always takes the initiative in communicating • holy—though he exists within creation, he is "other"—creation cannot be identified with him • passionate—God experiences holy love and anger • covenantally related to his creatures—God is loyal and binds himself in relationship • the source of meaning—the ultimate meaning of the world is found in the purposes of God • omnipotent—he is powerful beyond measure • worthy—of true worship
EVANGELIST	• savior and redeemer—he seeks out and saves that which is lost • gracious—the source of mercy and all gifts • abundant—his divine love flows out of his infinite abundance • the source of true joy—rejoices in himself • relational—he invites his creation into relationship • lover and elector —he pursues his people and purposes • sent—in himself, Jesus Christ, and the Spirit

Function	God is . . .
SHEPHERD	• Trinitarian—he exists in community-in-relationship • fully present—in all things • comforter—he has compassion and concerns himself with his creation • known in intimacy—he knows us and is involved with us in the here and now • righteous—he is in himself perfectly ordered and rightly related • merciful and forgiving—it is his nature to be merciful • love—and the ultimate lover • family—he is the divine parent; we are his children • shepherd—he reveals himself as a shepherd (Psalm 23, Psalm 80:1, Genesis 49:24)
TEACHER	• all-knowing—nothing is not known by him • logos (Word)—and the source of reason in human beings • glorious—he manifests himself in all things • prescient—he has direct knowledge and foreknowledge of all things • good and beautiful—and the source of all truth and beauty • whole and complete in himself—his "system" is perfectly and ecologically balanced • wise—he is the source of all wisdom and understanding

STOP

Awareness

Which of the fivefold roots of God do you most naturally relate to? Why do you think this is the case? Does it reflect your own base ministry, your past experience, your church culture, or something else?

How does a limited perception of God in relation to APEST affect your leadership and the culture you create around you?

Reflect back on your own personal faith journey. How has God impacted you at various points and revealed the fivefold attributes of his character?

Application

How could you choose to engage with one of the fivefold aspects of God that you are less familiar with?

How could you lead others in that process?

Who could you discuss and explore this with?

Look at table 2.2 above.

Think about a friend or colleague who isn't a Christian. Which of those aspects of God might be Good News to them? Share that with them!

APEST is Recapitulated by Jesus and Gifted to the Body of Christ

We are told that Jesus was "sent" by the Father in order to save, heal, restore, repair, and redeem a world that was broken through the original fall. Scripture tells us that he did this by becoming one of us, living as a full human being in a perfect way, and therefore recreating the human race in himself (Romans 5:12-21; Ephesians 2:1-22; Colossians 1:15-23; Hebrews 2:11-18). This is known as *recapitulation*. In becoming the new Adam, Jesus becomes the new *head* of the human race and is called the Head of his Body, the church. Christ as the new representative Man, the second Adam, succeeds where the first Adam failed and is therefore able to re-present, re-store, re-deem, and re-establish the godly basis of human life in the world. (In chapter three, we'll examine the way Jesus **perfectly lived out** APEST before giving it to the Body.)

So what does all this mean for 5Q? Ephesians 4:8–11 teaches that Jesus takes the pre-existing five-fold archetypes and (along with all the various other orders of creation) recapitulates them in true obedience to God. Jesus embodies APEST in a way that God originally intended, and in so doing he sanctifies the fallen archetypes. Having done this in his incarnation and cross, he then "gifts" them (Ephesians 4:7) to the Body of Christ, where they are embedded into the DNA of the church and subsequently lived out in different individuals in different times and places as their unique callings.

Seeing the Whole

In order to appreciate the full scope of APEST we need to keep the big picture in mind.

Let's put together what we've said so far, reordering it chronologically:

APEST is found in the nature and purposes of God
APEST is laced throughout Creation
APEST is active in society and culture
APEST is recapitulated by Jesus and gifted to the Body of Christ

so that . . .

The Body of Christ might attain to the fullness of Christ

Viewing APEST as a system helps us see the fivefold embedded into creation and culture, as well as envisioning a way for the Body of Christ to become mature. It also provides a paradigm for individual disciples to be able to grow and be effective both within the faith community and in their working week. APEST as a system becomes the lens through which we can help equip each person to become the most Christlike version of themselves and train them in the best example of their calling.[14]

Based on the above, we can also go on to say that APEST also provides us with a way to *identify* and *measure* the maturity of any *ecclesia*—the **marks of the church**. We'll explain this in chapter four so just hold onto it as a (significant) thought for now.

Take a look at the diagram below to get a sense of the full sweep of 5Q.

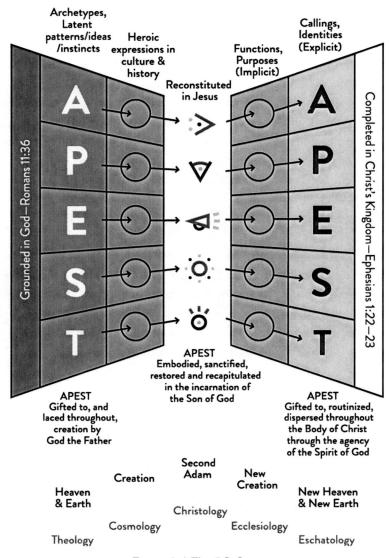

Figure 2.4 The 5Q System

NOTES

Key Headlines to Reflect On

Key Discussion Topics to Process

Key Action Points for Next Steps

3

J–APEST: The Fivefold Modes of Jesus' Presence in the Church

As we've already noted, Jesus redeemed, restored and re-established APEST through his perfect life, death and resurrection. By recapitulating all things in and through his life and ministry, Jesus becomes the perfect, quintessential expression of APEST. *His ministry can be summed up through these five purposes or functions.*

Before we go any further, let's remember a few important facts regarding the position and role of Jesus in the movement he started.

JESUS . . .

- is the full representation of God in the world (e.g., John 1:1–14; Colossians 1:15–20; Hebrews 1:1–3);
- shows us, and makes possible, a new way to relate to God (a new covenant);
- claims us as his own through his sacrificial death;
- establishes his unique role as the Mediator and High Priest, representing his people before the Father;
- is our Savior and Lord;
- creates a new humanity— the Body of Christ—in himself;
- sets the absolute standard for the church;
- is Founder and Finisher, Alpha and Omega.

And so the identity, purpose, and function of the church all centers on **who Jesus is** and **what he has done.** His life and teachings show us what it means to faithfully live in the Kingdom of God and we look to him to find out *who we are* (identity) and *what we are called to do* (purpose). Our authenticity is measured by the degree to which we *conform to, represent, and bear a living witness to the life, work, and teachings* of Jesus.

Demonstrating APEST for the Church

As followers of Jesus, we look to pattern ourselves after him, and it's therefore important to examine how Jesus lived out APEST. It is very clear from biblical accounts that Jesus is the perfect example of each of the APEST ministries.[15] Seeing Jesus in the light of the fivefold perspective helps us more fully appreciate the person and work of our Lord. In fact, his life would not be understandable without all five elements present:

- As Messiah, Jesus himself was sent into the world as the chosen agent of God's eternal mission. He followed the path that the Father had set for him. He reframed how God could be experienced and accessed; he extended the boundaries of God's kingdom on earth and initiated a worldwide movement that was to become known as Christianity. *He is the great Apostle.*

- Jesus was fiercely and uncompromisingly prophetic. Almost everything he said related to his covenantal faithfulness to God. He exposed the breakdown of the covenantal relationship with God's chosen people; he named injustice and railed against unrighteousness; he exposed the ungodly toxicity in misguided religion. He cast out demons, spoke truth to power, confronted evil and unrighteousness. *He is God's perfect Prophet.*

- Jesus proclaimed good news for the poor, forgiveness for all sinners, and salvation for the lost. Signs and wonders confirmed his witness. He opened the doors to all those previously excluded through religion and politics. The masses experienced him as genuine good news. Ultimately, he paid for this redemption with the sacrifice of his life. *He is the greatest Evangelist ever.*

- He worked to include the previously excluded people into the covenant community and in so doing created a new family, open to all who love Jesus. Everything about him radiated concern for people and for the establishment of true human community and relationships. His healings and his miracles demonstrated God's grace, mercy, and concern. *He is the perfect expression of the Shepherd, the Lover of his people.*

He taught people wherever and whenever he could. He chose, instructed, and guided disciples, teaching them his Way and the ways of the God of Israel. He actually recast the Torah by fulfilling it. His teachings were accessible to the simplest and the wisest alike. The medium of his life was its message: the Truth and Light. *He is the greatest Teacher ever.*

All five APEST functions are unmistakably present in Jesus' life and ministry. It's therefore not surprising that the New Testament gospel clearly has all these functions in them—mission/purpose, the prophetic call to repentance and relationship, the proclamation of good news of salvation, adoption into God's family, and direct access to the true knowledge of God.

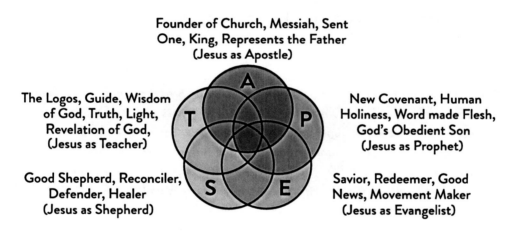

Founder of Church, Messiah, Sent One, King, Represents the Father (Jesus as Apostle)

The Logos, Guide, Wisdom of God, Truth, Light, Revelation of God, (Jesus as Teacher)

New Covenant, Human Holiness, Word made Flesh, God's Obedient Son (Jesus as Prophet)

Good Shepherd, Reconciler, Defender, Healer (Jesus as Shepherd)

Savior, Redeemer, Good News, Movement Maker (Jesus as Evangelist)

Figure 3.1 J-APEST: The Jesus-Shaped Expression of APEST

Viewing Jesus as the quintessential embodiment of the fivefold gives us a tangible example of how we should live as his Body.[16] This is an amazing gift to us; it means that through Jesus' perfect example, we can each find the perfect version of who we are called to be. And through the way that he lived, we are given a pattern and practices to help us grow as disciples in the way of Jesus. This is the practical nature of the grand call to be like Christ. Through the empowerment of the Holy Spirit, Jesus has concretely made a way for us to be like him as we live on this earth! This is not an abstract aspiration, but a *real example* of how we can walk out our calling in our lives. *Jesus shows us how to be the best version of ourselves.*

STOP

Awareness

In chapter five, Jon Ritner gives us a practical example of how we can pray the five modes of Christ's presence in our own lives. (See pages 96–98 for the full process.) He specifically applies this to his kids, but this could equally apply to ourselves, our team, our church or our organization.

As you read his example below, think about your own context: in which relationships could you apply the principle of praying the five modes of Christ's presence?

"At night, I pray through each of the five modes of Christ's presence in my kids' lives and in the life of our family. I try to filter the events and opportunities of the week through the five functions. I am amazed how each night the Spirit leads me to specific behaviors, character qualities, and habitual practices that I want to see become evident in our life as a family. As these prayers begin to bear fruit, I believe we will become a more effective example of Jesus and the Kingdom of God to the world around us."

Application

Begin to pray using the filter of the five modes of Christ's presence for your family, team or organization. Keep a prayer journal to see the impact of your prayers and to reflect on your learning.

From the MOX to the BOX to the FOX

As we have already noted, in Ephesians 4 we see Jesus giving APEST to the Body of Christ. To understand the significance of what has been given to the church, we need to briefly consider what the New Testament means by the "Body of Christ." The fact that we are called the *Body* of Christ indicates that there is a direct correspondence between the life and purpose of the church and the life, work, and mission of Jesus. We don't just simply *represent* Jesus; in some real way, we actually *embody* him. We *are* his literal hands, his literal feet, his literal heart. He chooses to live in and through his *ecclesia*. The church is therefore the *embodiment* of Christ. Dietrich Bonhoeffer went so far as to call the church "the form of Christ in the world."[17]

One simple way to remember the significance of APEST for the Body is through the acronyms, *MOX, BOX, FOX:*

The *ministry of Christ* (MOX)
is given to
the *Body of Christ* (BOX)
in order that
the church might reach the *fullness of Christ* (FOX).

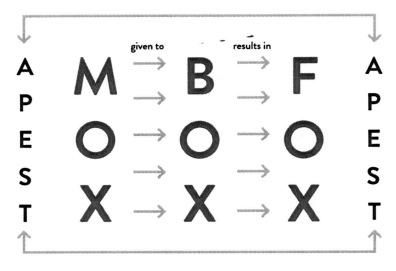

Figure 3.2 Ministry of Christ (MOX) Given to the Body of Christ (BOX)
which Results in the Fullness of Christ (FOX)

Putting the Last Pieces of the Puzzle Together

We're now clear that the Body of Christ exists to extend the ministry of Christ in the world. If Jesus expressed his ministry in terms of the fivefold, then *the church must also have all the fivefold functions operative to do what Jesus did and to attain to the fullness of Christ*. When we put it all together we can sense the amazing symmetry that Jesus has built into the Body. Table 3.1 below summarizes the full sweep of the 5Q system.

Table 3.1 5Q System in Overview

FUNCTION / CALLING:
APOSTOLIC / APOSTLE

Theological Roots (APEST in the doctrine of God)	Archetypes and Heroes (APEST patterns laced in and throughout creation)	Reconstituted APEST (Redeemed and exemplified in Jesus)	APEST Functions (Implicit) (Given to and coded into *ecclesia*)	APEST Callings (Explicit) (Practitioners)
Father, Creator, Sender, Sovereign, Designer, Judge, Source	Founder, General, Agent-envoy, Visionary, Pioneer, Adventurer **Examples:** Pioneers, Breakthrough designers, Innovators, Entrepreneurs, Visionaries, Embodiments of purpose-mission, Paradigm shifters, Cultural architects, Movement-makers, Systems thinkers, Business Leaders, Problem-Solvers, Imagineers, Start-ups	Founder, Messiah, Sent one, King/ Head, Messiah, God's kingdom agent, Establisher of genetic code/DNA, Establisher and builder of his church, Commissioner of his people	Organize around sentness, Maintain integrity of paradigm and DNA, Translocal networking, Entrepreneurial capacities, Church planting, Scale and scalability in organization, Innovation and risk-taking	Church planters, Innovators, Entrepreneurs, Cross-cultural missionaries, Organizational designers, Regional networkers, Cultural architects

FUNCTION / CALLING:
PROPHETIC / PROPHET

Theological Roots (APEST in the doctrine of God)	Archetypes and Heroes (APEST patterns laced in and throughout creation)	Reconstituted APEST (Redeemed and exemplified in Jesus)	APEST Functions (Implicit) (Given to and coded into ecclesia)	APEST Callings (Explicit) (Practitioners)
Holy, Faithful, Incarnate Transcendent, Covenantal, Just and True, Omnipotent	Seer, Warrior, Poet, Reformer, Iconoclast, Meaning-maker **Examples: Artists, Poets, Shamans, Ethicists, Activists, Liberators, Meaning-makers, Iconoclasts, Revolutionaries, Advocates, Existentialists, Anarchists, Hackers, Spiritualists, Mystics, Environmentalists, Whistle-blowers, Feminists, Aid workers, Psychologists, Politicians, Futurists, Quality controllers	Word made flesh, God's New Covenant, Faithful Son, Prophet (speaks and acts for/as God), Calls to repentance, The way/truth/light, Demonstrates perfect holiness and faithfulness, Speaks truth to power (both religious and secular), Radical ethics of the kingdom	Maintain God focus/ orientation, Require conformity to covenant obligations, Demonstrate right faith/fullness, Develop prefigurative community, Bring words of knowledge, Give prophetic insight	Intercessor, Social activists, Questioners of the status quo, Worship leaders, Holy rebels, Ethical leadership

FUNCTION / CALLING:

EVANGELISTIC / EVANGELIST

Theological Roots (APEST in the doctrine of God)	Archetypes and Heroes (APEST patterns laced in and throughout creation)	Reconstituted APEST (Redeemed and exemplified in Jesus)	APEST Functions (Implicit) (Given to and coded into ecclesia)	APEST Callings (Explicit) (Practitioners)
Savior, Redeemer, Gracious Giver, Lover, Merciful	Messenger, Achiever, Believer, Guerilla-leader, Champion, Storyteller **Examples:** Mobilizers, Recruiters, Negotiators, Sales, Media workers, Achievers, Marketers, Organizers, Miracle-workers, Communicators, Preachers, Dealers, Raconteurs, Journalists, Motivational speakers, Networkers, Buccaneers, Public relations	Savior, Message-messenger, Redeemer, The way/life, Proclaimer of the gospel, Embodies the gospel, Demonstrates the reign of God, Recruits followers, Bearer of love and hope (Israel's Messiah), Seeks and saves the lost	Recruit culture, Maintain commitment to Gospel theology and ethos, Invitational, Maintain cultural relevance, Inspirational	Recruiters to the movement, Storytellers, Spreaders of message (communicators), Apologists

FUNCTION / CALLING:

SHEPHERDING / SHEPHERD

Theological Roots (APEST in the doctrine of God)	Archetypes and Heroes (APEST patterns laced in and throughout creation)	Reconstituted APEST (Redeemed and exemplified in Jesus)	APEST Functions (Implicit) (Given to and coded into ecclesia)	APEST Callings (Explicit) (Practitioners)
Community in Trinity, Comforter, Immanent, Divine Parent, Compassionate	Caregiver, Defender, Peacemaker, Helper, Servant, Selfless, Healer Examples: Elders, Lovers, Guardians, Loyalists, Humanizers, Parents, First responders, Cultivators, Mediators, Military, Counselors, Health-workers, Priests, Community workers, Human resources, Police	Good Shepherd, Healer, Reconciler, Protector/Guardian of the community (lays down his life), The life, Reconciler, Healer, Establishes true community, God's righteous one	Cultivate loving and caring community, Protect members, Maintain relational glue, Develop pathways for maturity / discipleship, Create place of healing, Shalom	Pastoral carers, Spiritual directors, Community reconcilers, Relational glue, Healers-counselors, First responders

FUNCTION / CALLING:
TEACHING / TEACHER

Theological Roots (APEST in the doctrine of God)	Archetypes and Heroes (APEST patterns laced in and throughout creation)	Reconstituted APEST (Redeemed and exemplified in Jesus)	APEST Functions (Implicit) (Given to and coded into ecclesia)	APEST Callings (Explicit) (Practitioners)
Omniscient, Prescient, Truth, Beauty, Wisdom, Logos (Reason)	Sages, Thinkers, Observers, Philosophers, Guides, Scientists **Examples:** Coaches, Instructors, Investigators, Information workers, Professors, Educationalists, Mentors, Disciplers, Theoreticians, Debaters, Engineers, Researchers, Theologians, Accountants, Forensics, Legal workers	Rabbi, Logos, The truth, The way, Light of the world, Our teacher/guide, The Word made flesh, God's wise judge, The fulfillment of the Torah, The riches of knowledge and wisdom	Foster learning culture, Develop resources for learning, Articulate the theology-ideology for the group, Provide instruction in the Way	Instructors, Theologians, Philosophers, Guides, Writers, Thinkers, Truth-tellers

STOP

Awareness

Reflecting on your own APEST calling, review the table. What three things can you learn about God and what three things can you learn about yourself that are important for your maturity as a disciple and leader?

Reflect on your family, team or work colleagues. Using the tables above, think about some of the ways you could connect them to God, grow their maturity or release their God-given potential.

Application

Identify an area of weakness or deficit in your own fivefold maturity or an area you'd like to grow in. Identify who you could approach to learn from and what practices you could put in place daily or weekly to mature.

Create a vision statement for your 5Q maturity six months and eighteen months from now. Where will you have grown? How will you have deepened and developed as a disciple and leader? What will your relationships look like? How will you be expressing more of the fullness of Christ in and through your life?

Create a plan for the next month and semester of various ways you will invest in three key relationships to help them grow in their 5Q maturity and express more of the fullness of Christ.

NOTES

Key Headlines to Reflect On

Key Discussion Topics to Process

Key Action Points for Next Steps

4

Marking the Body: Becoming the Church of Our Dreams!

We have now seen that APEST is given to the *Body of Christ* by Jesus and that these are expressed in five purposes/functions given to the whole church and expressed in the callings of individuals in various contexts. We are now going to take things even deeper and look at how the fivefold provides us with one of the most accurate ways of *identifying* the church and *measuring* its maturity and effectiveness. This book and its associated tests are geared around this concept, so we will elaborate on this as we go. But for now, let's start with some definitions.

Is it a Church? Is It a Pub? Is it a Mosque . . .

So, how *do* we know when a church is a church? How is the church different from the local pub, the sports club, or the mosque? How do we recognize a group of people as Jesus' Body and Bride? The answer must somehow revolve around the fact that the Body is the group of people who express the life and ministry of Jesus.

"The marks of the church" help us to differentiate the church from any other community and indicate whether or not a congregation is authentic and a genuine church of Jesus Christ. The marks are the *defining characteristics*, the *distinguishing functions*, and the *observable features* that mark us off as different. So, first let's look at what have been known as the official marks of the church in Western church history, before we go on to suggest APEST as valid marks of the church.

First consider the Roman Catholic marks, derived from the Nicene Creed: They state that the true church of Jesus Christ is *one, holy, catholic,* and *apostolic,* and that these elements must be visibly present and observable. For example, to be truly one and catholic, there must be visible unity of structure and confession. For the Roman church, this means submission to Catholic sacraments, leadership, and structure, as there is no other church than the one with the Catholic sacraments. Apostolic succession, the papacy, the magisterium, and other Catholic dogma likewise come into play.

However inadequate the Catholic marks might appear, the Protestant marks are even more deficient. In order to distinguish the Protestant movement from the Catholic church, the Protestant Reformers concluded that there are only two (or three) marks of the church: the right preaching of God's Word and the right administration of the ordinances/sacraments—baptism and the Lord's Supper.[18] So according to Protestant theology, a true church can be identified by the practice of the two sacraments and biblical preaching. Talk about an underwhelming description of the movement that Jesus started! We doubt even Jesus would recognize that as an *ecclesia*![19]

That's a big call. Why do we say this?

Firstly, it's what's *left out* of these Protestant marks that really matters. There doesn't necessarily need to be an explicit mention of God, Jesus, or the Holy Spirit to be considered an observable mark/metric—they would be pretty tricky to measure anyhow—but whatever happened to a metrics defined by concrete expressions of love, discipleship, evangelism, mission, service, worship, or community? Not only are these not mentioned in the traditional marks, they are not even implied! The traditional marks leave us all with the strong impression that preaching and the practice of the two sacraments in a Sunday service are all that is required for us to be a church, because these are the only things being measured![20] There are glaring holes in this depiction of the church.

Secondly, these marks seem to require an ordained priest to deliver the sacraments and do the necessary preaching. Though protestants formally insist on the priesthood of all believers, our practice often suggests otherwise.

Thirdly, it seems that the only place we can actually come into contact with the sacraments/ordinances is in a Sunday gathering of the church—and this would only happen intermittently because not all sacraments are practiced every Sunday. By tying the sacraments to formal gatherings to be conducted only by ordained clergy we have effectively "institutionalized grace" and locked it up in a stained-glass institution. This clearly runs counter to Jesus' explicit teaching that worship can no longer be limited to a specific location and even less a building (John 4:20-24).

How can we possibly have used these marks to define the people of God? If our vision of the church and its ministry really comes to this—to the orderly administration of churchly sacraments, pulpit preaching, and perhaps some discipline—then all we can say is, "God help us!"

Jesus to the Rescue

So how can the APEST typology help us define the church? We've already noted that Jesus is the central, defining, mark of the church—everything else flows from this center. He is our Savior, and he is also our Lord. That means that anything that is to be called his Body is required to look like him, otherwise it is not *his* Body. He is the absolute standard of everything that has to do with the church, as both its Lord and its example. If the church claims to be Jesus' Body, then it must look like him and bear his marks. The lack of those marks indicates the degree to which Jesus is not Lord of any given church.

Let's now link this with APEST. We have already seen how Jesus redeems the fallen fivefold archetypes, perfectly embodying and reconstituting them and how he then gives them to his church. Jesus, in his perfect humanity is the most perfect and full expression of the fivefold in all history: he is J-APEST, *the* exemplary expression of APEST. By seeing his ministry through the lens of APEST, we can begin to understand the ministry that he then gives to the church. As we have already stated, **APEST is the ministry of Christ expressing itself through the Body of Christ.**

And as we have also seen, APEST is also the means by which the church "attains to" the fullness of Christ, integrates and "becomes mature." APEST are, in effect, five functions or purposes "given" to the church itself. If they are the purposes given to the church, then they must be identified and developed if we are going to fulfill our calling as the Body of Christ.

Once we have "seen" the APEST system, the next step of understanding the fivefold marks of the church is simple and natural.

If the Body of Christ is to *follow the example of Christ* and if APEST is the *mode of Christ's presence* among his people, then we can logically say that the authenticity of a church can be measured by *the presence and expression of APEST.*

We can therefore say that the true church is expressed in the following characteristics or marks:

- **Jesus: The founding mark:** The community that belongs to Jesus—the people called, sanctified, redeemed, by the Father through his chosen Messiah, Jesus. By the power of God's Spirit, the church exists to represent Jesus, to imitate him, to live out every aspect of his message, and to extend his kingdom. The authentic church is measured by the degree to which Jesus is present and revered. (*Jesus as the founding mark defines and serves as a foundation for all the rest.*)

- **The apostolic mark:** The people-movement that participates in the redemptive and trans-formative mission of God in the world. The true church experiences and seeks to live out its sentness (*missio*) in every way possible. Therefore, when a community engages apostolically in God's mission of transforming the world, it is authentically church.

- **The prophetic mark:** The holy people that stands for God in the world. When a community stands up for covenantal justice and calls all to the covenant love of God, to true worship, obedience to God and his word, repentance, and to prayer, it is authentically church.

- **The evangelistic mark:** The Body of saved people that joyfully proclaim the good news and call all to experience freedom and salvation in and through Jesus. The church is the witness to, as well as a demonstration of, the presence of good news in the world. A community arising from the good news of salvation is authentically church.

- **The shepherding mark:** The family of God's redeemed people that nurtures a faithful, reconciled community that witnesses to the Resurrection through its common life. When a community represents God's chosen, reconciled and reconciling, healed and healing family in the world, then it is authentically church.

- **The teaching mark:** The wise and intelligent people that passionately seek truth and share all the treasures of the wisdom, insight, and knowledge of God hidden in Christ Jesus, faithfully nurturing understanding and communicating truth in the world. When the knowledge of God is sought, treasured, and shared, there is an authentic church.

Wherever you have the kind of people described above; where **all five marks** built on the foundation of Jesus as the founding mark are demonstrably present—missional impact, covenant faithfulness, gospel proclamation, reconciled community, and deep wisdom—there, brothers and sisters, you have a real, authentic church! Church as Jesus meant it to be, made of colorful, beautiful living stones.

Just imagine the holistic transformation that would occur if the church fully embraced all five functions:

	Mature Expression of *Ecclesia* (Mark)	The (Desired) Social Impact
Apostolic	Church as theologically consistent, missionally engaged in all of life, culturally dynamic, high impact, organizationally adaptive, scalable, and a church planting movement.	• A transformed society • Gospel saturation • A church unified in purpose and mission
Prophetic	Church as alternative society (a prefigurative community), with strong commitment to worship, prayer, spiritual warfare, holiness, justice, and incarnational witness.	• A restored community • A community/society living in covenant relationship to God • Respect for God's presence
Evangelistic	Church is an experience of Good News. It is a redemptive, infectious, culturally relevant, and always hopeful, people movment.	• A redeemed community • A growing movement • A thriving society built on restored relation to God • A grace economy built on sharing
Shepherding	Church is a human community that is reconciled, healed, forgiven, which expresses itself in loving relationships.	• A reconciled community • Loving human community • Reconciled across race, gender, age, nationality • A communion in Christ
Teaching	Church is a well-practiced community of learners with increasing self-awareness, understanding, and presenting wisdom for living well.	• A wise community • The Kingdom of Truth • Loving God with mind, soul, strength

Table 4.1 The Five Marks of the Church and Their Desired Social impact

STOP

Awareness

How does using APEST as valid marks of the church expand your thinking?

What's your present reality? Using each of the marks, reflect on what is growing, strong, struggling or absent?

Application

How could your group, church or organization grow in each of the five marks?

Pick one of the marks and form a plan for intentional investment, prayer and practice to grow this aspect over the next three months.

Who will you process this plan with to put it in to practice?

(These processes will prepare you well for taking the Systems and Diagnostic tests—see the appendix—and working with the results.)

And so we see that the purpose of APEST in the Body is not only so we might mature and have a missional ministry equal to our missional task, but also to provide us with **visible markers as to the authenticity of our expression.** We are now in a position to be able to picture what it means for a church to be functional or dysfunctional.

It should be relatively easy to now see that the church's problems stem from what is left out or missing from the APEST system. If one or more of the marks are removed or significantly diminished, the result is a proportionally and correspondingly dysfunctional church. When is a church a true church? When it actively demonstrates its participation in *all* the fivefold functions/purposes to some degree or another. A community that does not have all five marks evident is a community on its way to being a true church, or on its way out.

For instance, if a church is strong in evangelism and teaching, but meaningfully lacks the others, then the best we can call it is a "parachurch" that evangelizes through apologetics and theology. But as it does not engage in corporate worship, new church planting, prayer-justice and discipleship, it is not an *ecclesia* as the New Testament would define it.

Or, in another example, a church that fails to engage with the mission of God in the world misses a fundamental part of its unique purpose to be a partner and agent of the Kingdom of God. It will make no effort to go beyond its own culture, will not multiply, and will remain or become a static institution rather than a dynamic movement. Without apostolicity alongside all the other marks, we cannot ever be a true and authentic church.

A church that fails to create and nurture genuine healing community, and that doesn't care for all people irrespective of class, race, gender, and so on, is likely to result in a rather toxic, immature, judgmental and unloving nest of people. If we remove shepherding as a mark of authentic *ecclesia*, the resulting church is guaranteed to become just another dis-eased, wounding, and even hateful religion.

Any significant asymmetry in the APEST typology creates a kind of imbalanced fanaticism that sees the answer in a singular function rather than in fivefold symphony. For instance, a prophet believing that more emphasis on prophetic functions is the answer to the church's problems is likely to create a group of people who end up engaging in mass groupthink. Precisely this has happened so often in church history. Too many significant movements have been derailed by imbalanced leaders with an over-emphasis on one of the fivefold.

The church is more authentic when there is a healthy demonstration of **all** the marks. The *fullness* of Christ is when all the functions are *fully* operative. In other words, the shaded in portion in figure 4.1 below is the "Jesus-space"—the zone of Jesus' operative presence in the ministry of the church.

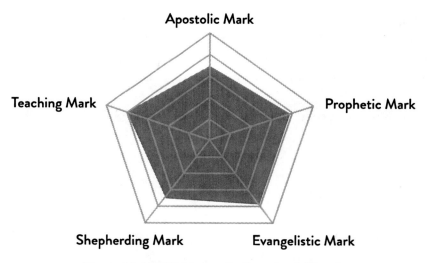

Figure 4.1 APEST Marks of a Functional Church

Correspondingly, the church is increasingly inauthentic, and dysfunctional, the fewer marks it exhibits. This will be evident by the lack of proportion or symmetry in the pattern. The 5Q ("Jesus-space") in figure 4.2 is much smaller and disproportional. Sadly, this pattern would probably describe the average evangelical congregation in North America, where there is a single pastor whose primary role is to teach, preach and offer pastoral counselling (ST).

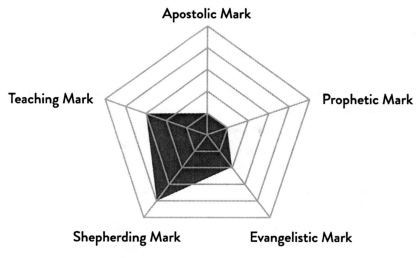

Figure 4.2 APEST Marks of a Dysfunctional Church

What about the apostolic, prophetic, and evangelistic functions? What about innovation, vision, and an entrepreneurial spirit? What about prayer and intercession, worship as a lifestyle? What about reaching the community and bringing a compelling message of the gospel?

Those are obviously underdeveloped or missing altogether. And you can be assured their lack is felt.

A church that is more of a contemporary megachurch may look like figure 4.3.

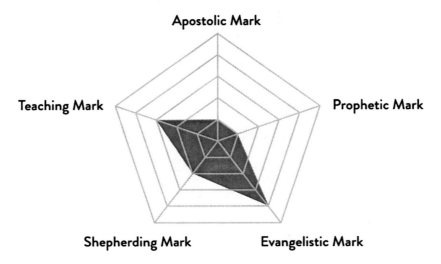

Figure 4.3 Graphical Depiction of an ETs church

What about the apostolic, prophetic, and shepherding functions that are necessary for healthy ministry? How are people cared for individually and specifically? What about social justice issues, challenging consumerism, or speaking truth to power? Certainly, such a church might have vision for growth, but what about training and releasing leaders to start their own movements and not just satellite churches or communities?

Hopefully you get the point by now. All five functions are needed and are based on Jesus' presence and example at the center. This is what it means to be the Body of Christ—the embodiment of Christ in the world.

Adopting APEST as marks of the church helps us to live into our collective calling, and we must be willing to reconfigure the way we do church accordingly.

We can use a similar process to assess a leadership team. One person is unlikely to have a full spectrum of the fivefold—we all have different strengths and weaknesses. A healthy team ought to reflect a healthy symmetry in terms of APEST so that as a whole team they more fully represent the ministry of Jesus. When the full expressions of the APEST capacities are valued in an organization, each person on the leadership team is empowered to best use his or her gifts. In figure 4.4 below, we see the blended personal profiles of four individuals. Though there is still room for growth, we can see that in this blended profile there is a good representation of each of the fivefold.

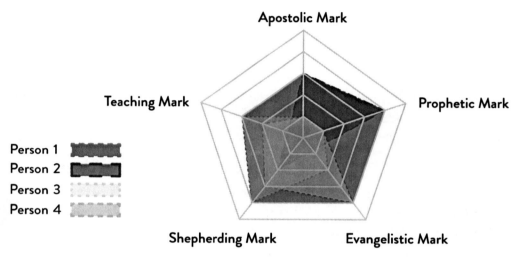

Figure 4.4 Graphical Depiction of a Blended Profile

Evaluation before Application

Now that you have an understanding of 5Q, it might be tempting to jump straight to application. But there is an important, and often undervalued, stage before moving to application: the need to evaluate your organization's current expression of the fivefold.

During the twentieth century it was discovered, in both science and psychology, that the simple act of measuring something changes it. Someone asks you where your big toe is *right now*; you wiggle it to identify where it is. But you have moved it in order to locate it, and that process moves it from where it was when the question was asked. If the question had not been asked, you would not have moved your toe. The act of trying to measure something inherently changes it.

To help in the evaluation process, we have developed two specific tests to help churches and organizations accurately measure their current expression of APEST as well as assess their depth of awareness, understanding, and application of it throughout the organization. These can be downloaded at www.5qcentral.com/tests/ and a more detailed explanation of the tests can be found in the appendix.

We strongly encourage you and your team to take the tests; they will be an invaluable investment for the life of your organization and will help you more accurately reflect on where further growth is required and therefore help identify a more specific action plan and identify what tools are required.

The **5Q Diagnostic** is designed to give a snapshot of your organization's expression of the five-fold intelligences. It is designed to help you see what is currently active or present in your organization.

The **5Q Systems Analysis** is a more advanced test that measures the levels of organizational awareness and maturity in APEST thinking. Built on the framework of stages of maturity and learning it not only assesses the active presence of 5Q in the church, as the straightforward diagnostic does, but also the depth of awareness, understanding, and application of it throughout the organization.

The **APEST Vocational Profiles** provide the only statistically verified instrument available. Based on the definitions found in this book and in Alan's other books on APEST, these assessments (solo and 360) give you a picture of the unique personal shape of your ministry.

(All are available at www.5qcentral.com/tests/)

NOTES

Key Headlines to Reflect On

Key Discussion Topics to Process

Key Action Points for Next Steps

SECTION TWO

EQUIP
(THE TOOLS AND TACTICS)

Introduction

You should now have a good understanding of the key ideas of 5Q. If you haven't yet taken the tests to evaluate how your organization is functioning, now is the time to do it! As we mentioned on page 69, evaluating your current organizational expression of the fivefold is an invaluable investment. Take a look at the appendix for more details and go to www.5qcentral.com/tests/ to download the tests.

Now it's time for the rubber to hit the road! It's time to apply your knowledge. You'll remember from section one, that we defined 5Q as the ability to:

Recognize and *understand* APEST in the broadest and deepest way possible, in creation, culture and the Body of Christ (Awareness)

and

Live out and *release* the fullness and maturity of the ministry of Jesus in our own and other people's lives. (Application)

In order to have high 5Q, it's not simply enough to recognize and understand the full extent and capacities of APEST. Our knowledge and understanding must be activated and applied symphonically to bring about maturity and fullness in the Body of Christ.

Remember the story of the wise and foolish builders? If you grew up in church, no doubt you sang about it in Sunday School. Jesus starts the story with an important statement:

Everyone who hears these words of mine [awareness] and puts them into practice [application] is like a wise man who built his house on the rock.

Matthew 7:24

We are called to be obedient and to act upon the things that God shows us. That's why in the book of James, we are reminded to *put into practice what we have heard*. Look at the verses below, taking note of the italicized words and phrases which emphasize the importance not only of hearing the information but of applying it.

Do not *merely listen* to the word, and so deceive yourselves. *Do* what it says. Anyone who listens to the word but *does not do* what it says is like someone who looks at his face in a mirror and, after looking at himself, goes away and immediately *forgets* what he looks like. But whoever looks intently into the perfect law that gives freedom, and *continues* in it—*not forgetting* what they have heard, but *doing* it—they will be blessed in what they *do*.

James 1:22–25 (our italics)

We might be an expert in APEST, holding a comprehensive understanding of the meaning and implications of each of the fivefold. But unless we put that into practice in our own lives and in helping those whom we lead to put it into practice, then it is fruitless. This section is intended to help you live out 5Q in your own life and in the lives of those you lead.

STOP

Awareness

Reflect on your own awareness and application. Which is generally your stronger side—awareness or application? What would it look like to use your strength to benefit others in your team or context? How could you invest and grow in your weaker side?

Application

What are two things you could do differently next week that would help you grow in your awareness?

What are two things you could do differently next week that would help you grow in your application?

5

Tools and Tactics

The best way to ensure ideas have impact is to embed them into the very rhythms and habits of community, in the form of common tools, tactics and practices. A tool is a mental device or physical implement used to perform an operation necessary in the practice of a vocation or profession. Each tool delivers a distinct function, (e.g., a saw is for cutting wood, a hammer for nails). A tactic is the most efficient or effective way to use that tool and a way to grow in your craftsmanship and confidence with the tool itself.

Each of the tools suggested below will similarly deliver a certain impact, like changing and developing thinking, culture, practices, and so on. Each of the tactics noted will help you to grow in your awareness and application of 5Q within your context. A good craftsman has numerous tools and knows what each can and cannot do. Knowing which tools are available, understanding the task at hand, and having some clarity about the desired outcome, should determine the choice of the tool and the tactic of how it should be used.

Because each of these tools focuses on a different dimension of APEST we highly recommend you try as many of them as possible. However, we believe you will find that each of these will be useful at different times, and in different parts of the process. Get your teams trying these out.

Each of the tactics will give you and your team the opportunity to identify and realize 5Q potential more effectively in the people and places of your context. We'd encourage you to reflect on and process these tactics together as a team to learn and grow through reflective practice and experiential learning.

As you begin to engage with these tools and tactics, you may find that you would benefit from additional insight and experience. To address this, we've created a training process with experienced

5Q practitioners who can be an outside voice and additional investment for you to grow in 5Q maturity as a team or organization (find the 5Q collective at www.5Qcentral.com).

Before you start any exercise below, be sure that each member of the group understands the basic definitions and how each of the fivefold functions/callings is distinct from the others in purpose, competencies, motivation, primary insight, and outcome. (Turn to page 3 for a reminder of the APEST definitions.) For instance, don't confuse evangelistic work with apostolic just because it looks entrepreneurial. Each participant should be able to know the broad difference between apostolic and evangelistic profiles and not be confused by entrepreneurialism, which can in fact serve all functions.[21]

Tools

Personal APEST Portrait

The first tool will focus on developing a "portrait," or profile, of each person's particular calling by associating the APEST on a descending order. The best way to get a statistically verified picture of your vocational shape or portrait is to simply do the test online (www.5qcentral.com/tests). However, it is an enriching process when it is also done as a dynamic group process of communal discernment. So we highly recommend both test and process.

Personal Processing
In order to honor how God calls and shapes people, there needs to be some deep personal reflection. And so each member of the group is to do the following exercise before coming together in the group.

- Paul says in Ephesians 4:7 that each one of us has been given a measure of gifting from Christ. When you think about the measure of gifting that Christ has given you in each of the five APEST ministries, and what you know about the agreed definitions of APEST (see page 3), what would you say is your primary or dominant calling? What about your secondary calling? Fill out the graph below with the primary APEST gifting in the largest circle, your secondary in the next largest circle, and so on. What does this say about you? Think of events and meetings in your own life that connect to your profile.

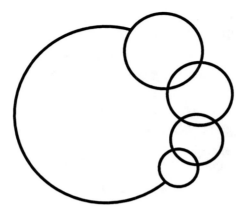

Figure 5.1 APEST Personal Profile

- Once you have filled in the circles, take the online test at www.5qcentral.com/tests (optional but recommended) to correct or confirm the insights gained from the above exercise.

- Journal the insights that you gain from the exercise and bring them to share with the group.

The Group Process

When you come together as a group, create the necessary social conditions for each member to be able to share for up to thirty minutes. If you need to take a few meetings to get through the entire group, this ought to be seen as a valuable investment of time.

- Each member should *describe their portrait*; how they feel about it; and why they believe it to be an accurate reflection of their personal calling. In other words, let them share their story, their sense of calling, their defining experiences, and perhaps where their vocational passions lie. To model this, we suggest the leader goes first because people will have some experience of his or her fivefold profile.

- Then the rest of the group is invited to give *honest but loving feedback* regarding the portrait. Is it correct? Can the community confirm what the individual is saying? How, if at all, can it be adjusted? The important thing to realize here is that people receive honest feedback regarding the nature of their influence on others. Because APEST is called a Body dynamic, we will only really know ourselves in relation to the other members of the Body of Christ. The truth is we cannot know ourselves in isolation from others; we can only know ourselves in relation to others—in community. This is an important aspect of the teaching about the Body of Christ in Ephesians as well as Corinthians.

- *Adjust the portrait accordingly*: Having heard the loving feedback of others, by submitting himself/herself to Body feedback, the person under review might need to adjust their individual profile accordingly.

- *The group prays for, and affirms the calling, of that person* and encourages them toward greater self-awareness and impact.

APEST Perspectives

Mark Conner, one of Alan's friends from Australia, places an object (say, a statue) in the middle of a round table and asks people to share what they see. He notes that two things happen. First, everyone sees the object differently. Second, no one sees it accurately, since each only sees it from where he or she sits. Consequently, the only way everyone can see the object accurately is when each person listens to everyone else's perspective.

This exercise demonstrates that without multiple perspectives, we cannot develop an accurate view of the challenges and opportunities in front of us. This is true in every area of life and ministry—for problem-solving, decision-making, vision creation, and strategic planning.

The APEST Perspectives tool simply puts an idea, topic, problem, or subject at the center of the conversation and then invites each of the people present to describe what they see from within their predominant vocations, or from within the logic of the functions they represent. So for instance, if you put the term *gospel* at the center of the diagram below, how do you think an apostle's perspective might be different from, say, a shepherd's? What aspects would each of the APEST highlight? Now put the term *church* at the center, or *culture, organization, spirituality,* and so on.

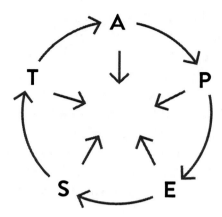

Figure 5.2 APEST Perspectives

If you're reading this book as a church leader, we'd recommend you put your core values through this process with your core staff, board/eldership and key leaders. Values help shape culture (whereas vision sets direction) and using this process and engaging the APEST perspective in this way will help your church to more maturely, holistically, and creatively express those values.

You can also use this tool for problem-solving, thinking through strategy, culture creation, planning, communication, key messaging, etc. It is also very useful for each team member to understand and respect the opinions of others and the perspectives from beyond their dominant gifting.

Base and Phase

The aim of this tool is to help identify areas that need development in each of us and to prompt leadership to design a process by which all move toward maturity. 3DM, a movement that stems from the work of Mike and Sally Breen, developed "Basing and Phasing" as a great process by which everyone can become more aware of the Body dynamics of APEST and learn about themselves at the same time. Whilst the "base" was identified as an individual's primary APEST gifting, it was recognized that an individual would also experience particular "phases" in ministry, during which they would operate more distinctly in one of the remaining four APEST. The churches they led always saw the phase time as a time for learning provided at the prompting of the Holy Spirit to help each disciple learn more about leadership and ministry, and as an equipping necessary for the ministry and season that individuals found themselves in. As such, the base-phase process was more than just a tool; it was understood as the work of the Spirit in the life of the church to help develop maturity.[22]

Paul says the overarching purpose of APEST is maturity, and that maturity happens through the process of equipping. As Tim Catchim and Alan say in *The Permanent Revolution*, the word Paul uses in Ephesians 4:12 for "equip" was in some cases used to describe the mending of torn fishing nets, while in other cases it was used to describe the process of setting a broken bone. Overall, the word carries the idea of increasing one's ability to function in a certain area. Paul is telling us that God gives each person APEST gifts so each individual in the Body of Christ can increase his or her ability to function within the five categories of Christ's ministry.

We all have a base ministry in which we feel most comfortable. This base ministry flows out of our primary gifting. In order to mature, we have to enter a phase where we receive training and experience in one of the other four ministries. It would look something like this:

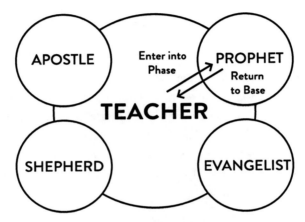

Figure 5.3 APEST Base and Phase

So, for example, teachers are not just designed for teaching. Everyone has all five APEST giftings to various degrees; maturity and fullness in Jesus comes as we move toward all five in us. For a teacher (T), growing toward maturity means learning to also function in the other four primary categories of ministry (APES).

Fill out the diagram below (figure 5.4), putting your base (primary) ministry in the middle of the largest circle. Based on life experience, write down which particular APEST ministries you have entered into—phases of equipping within the smaller circles. Then, with a few words, describe your growth experience in the box beside each phase.

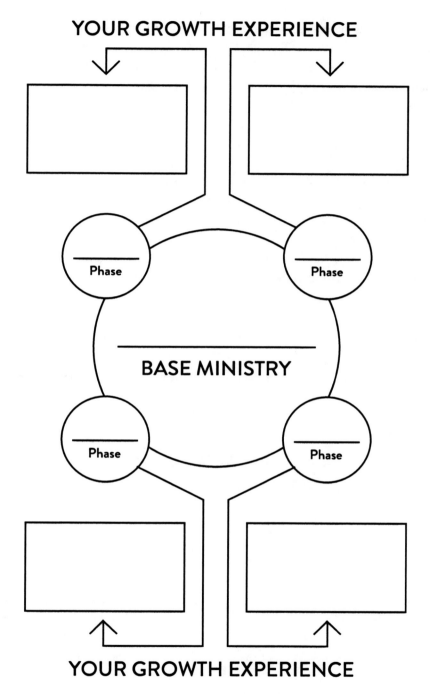

Figure 5.4 Base and Phase Exercise

We are often not the ones who orchestrate a phase in our life; instead, circumstances or a relationship typically guide us into it. The goal is not to agonize about your deficits or lack of experience in the various APEST ministries, but to remain open to entering a phase and to embrace it when it happens. If the opportunity does not present itself, we can always seek out opportunities to learn from others.

Analyzing Your Journey of APEST

Reflecting on our own journey of development can be helpful in terms of evaluating progress, identifying gaps, reflecting on who we've learned from and how we've learned, as well as considering how we might use what we've learned to disciple others. Take a minute and consider your APEST journey and what you have learned. What functions in each of the areas of APEST do you know something about? How have you learned that? It can be encouraging to see how God has been faithful in our lives. It can also help us see how adding a little intentionality to our discipleship processes can help us begin to develop a leadership pipeline.

Table 5.1 Analyzing Your Journey of APEST

	Apostolic	Prophetic	Evangelistic	Shepherding	Teaching
When? *When have you been developed in this?*					
Where? *What vocational role were you serving in?*					
What? *What APEST functions were you growing in?* *(See table 1.1 on page 7 for the various functions.)*					

	Apostolic	Prophetic	Evangelistic	Shepherding	Teaching
Who? *Who was helping you, mentoring you, or equipping you in this?*					
How? *What method of development did that person or God use to grow you in that area?*					
Was this an intentional equipping process?					

APEST Pipeline

In this exercise, the team can work to grow the skills and competencies of a leader within a particular APEST function and develop integration, with all leaders growing in awareness and appreciation of the other APEST functions.

To begin, the team needs to construct a profile of what they think each APEST calling should look like as it grows in competency and integration. Paint a picture of a competent practitioner of each of the callings and imagine each of the fivefold working intentionally with each other. What mentality, behaviors, skills, and competencies would they possess and how would they demonstrate an engagement and partnership with the other four functions?

As with a real pipeline, it is also important to consider where the blockages, gaps, silos or leaks are, so the process should also involve anticipating what the particular stress points or struggles will be for each of the APEST in the training process.

Once clarified, the team then develops a model process (which includes a sense of the curriculum/content that would be needed and a training process) in order to disciple people into the ideal. In other words, what would the discipleship or apprenticeship process look like in each of the five categories? Leaders are trained *together* as a leadership group so they have a growing awareness of all of the fivefold as they are trained alongside each other. They are also trained *specifically* so they are sharpened and grow in their fivefold function intentionally.

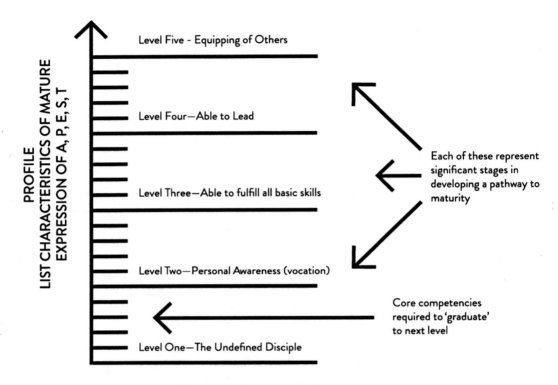

Figure 5.5 Competency-Based Process

The process developed ought to be articulated in terms of what is needed to acquire the competencies in a leader's particular fivefold and to grow in active partnership with the other fivefold functions. Theory is passed on through coaching and practice, until each student can demonstrate mastery of the task or competency required. Because each person is more than a single fivefold (each person actually has all five at varying strengths), once a person has reached the competency of their current track, they should go through at least one more additional track. This is how the Base-and-Phase tool can be combined with the APEST Pipeline. Learning is done alongside others so the student grows in awareness of all five from interaction with others. This is important because it is closer to the process of discipleship itself. If you wish, you can use the outline in figure 5.5 as a process for the team.

An APEST pipeline gives the opportunity to develop the APEST callings and functions within a 5Q framework but it also means that APEST training can be tailored to suit the particular purposes and context of an organization. This means the training can be personalized but not individualistic i.e., training with the intention of bringing the organization to maturity, not just investing in an individual.

Do this for all the APEST profiles. Below is an example of what this could look like at Level Two and Level Three leadership (as referred to in figure 5.5):

Leadership Development (Level Two)—Personal Awareness
Competency and skill to learn at this level—Growth in self-awareness and competency

Apostle: Mobilizing people toward action and pioneering new missional frontiers
Prophet: Helping everyone hear and know truth, and creating a depth and integrity of culture
Evangelist: Encouraging and equipping people to share, and speaking/ sharing the gospel
Shepherd: Loving others into fullness of life, and demonstrating the love of God to those who don't know him
Teacher: Creating depth and maturity in the word of God, and creating access points to truth and for truth to be expressed to those that don't know God

Leadership Focus (Level Three)—Able to fulfill basic skills
Competency and skill to learn at this level—Intentionality of the leaders' resources (time, money and effort) to primarily be invested in

Apostle: Impact (design, momentum, new ground broken)
Prophet: Faithfulness (in action, of people and culture)
Evangelist: Communication (offering of invitation and engagement of people)
Shepherd: Inclusion (depth of care and engaging with freedom)
Teacher: Learning (systematic and thorough engagement with truth)

On the diagram below (figure 5.6), the vertical journey (as detailed above) is the journey to greater competency and the horizontal journey is the journey to greater awareness and appreciation.

Once this training process is complete, you will not only have conceptualized a pretty potent agenda for discipleship, but you will have developed a pipeline for leadership development and activation (see figure 5.6) and a strong leadership culture where appreciation and awareness is high within your leadership group.

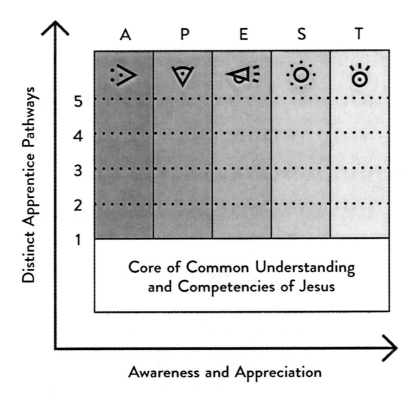

Figure 5.6 Competency-Based Training System

APEST Training Environments

As we begin to engage with 5Q not only personally but as a leader, we need to consider how we will enable those within our sphere of influence, and the organization itself, to embark on the journey of change. As a whole organization engages with APEST thinking (in terms of both functions and callings), we need to inform people well and train leaders effectively.

When training leaders within an organization there are three primary environments to consider:

- **Classroom:** creating teaching environments where input around APEST occurs for each individual calling and function, as well as general APEST overview. A disciple can then hear and learn the information about APEST and individual calling and functions. This is an essential part of the learning and training process (the classic "program" model employed by most churches) but is ineffective if it is the only part of the process, as in so many cases.

- **Apprenticeship:** creating relational training processes so that leaders who are more mature in their fivefold callings and functions are encouraging, empowering and equipping those with the same calling and function (e.g., an apostle training another apostle). Mature leaders can also apprentice those with a different APEST "base" or calling (e.g., an apostle training a teacher to grow in apostolic mindset and behavior). This apprenticeship and attentiveness process grows confidence, character and competency.

- **Immersion:** creating experiences where disciples are able to experience an environment where one of the functions is overtly expressed and the leading beat in setting culture and practice. In this experience, they can interpret the "feel" of a predominantly prophetic environment, for example. Immersion is also valuable to experience environments where there is a healthy fivefold balance so that some of the 5Q symphony and synergy can be experienced first-hand. This immersion process creates space for intuitive and experiential learning.

Utilizing the classroom (teaching program), apprenticeship (training process) and immersion (experiential learning) are all vital for a fruitful engagement for your leaders. Each of these three can provide experience, equipping, and empowering around 5Q.

APEST Culture

As an organization starts the 5Q journey and begins to perceive the symphony of 5Q, it can then engage with the component parts. Every organization is made up of culture and structure. We often make the mistake of attending to the structure and ignoring the culture. The stages outlined below will help identify the starting point for your community's APEST culture as it engages with 5Q.

Calling is about playing our part personally as we engage with the fivefold, and function is about partnership and purpose amongst and alongside others to edify the Body and extend the Kingdom. So a 5Q understanding helps us mature and move forward together.

Below are the different levels to assess the *understanding, engagement, expression* and *multiplication* of APEST. The levels grow toward a process of maturity. A healthy culture expressing APEST culture well will have all seven layers present.

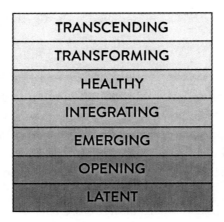

Figure 5.7 APEST Culture Building Blocks

- **Latent**: are all five *even considered?*
    - Occasional conversation or discussion of APEST
    - A few in the organization engaged with APEST
    - Some active APEST functions expressed but mostly unrecognized and not acknowledged as APEST

- **Opening**: are all five *being explored?*
    - Biblical truth and principles being explored, studied and initial engagement within the core leadership
    - A small number of healthy APEST examples present in the organization
    - Questions being asked and active dialogue is occurring within the organization

- **Emerging**: are all five *understood?*
    - Biblical truth and principles engaged and understood within the organization
    - APEST is validated across the organization
    - Healthy APEST examples are present in the organization and across each level of the organization

- **Integrating**: are all five *voiced?*
    - Pursuing intentionally; not accidental or reactionary; diversity and a healthy spread of APEST across the organization
    - Each APEST celebrated for their identity and contribution to the organization

- Each APEST empowered and given a "voice" to speak into the culture and structure of the organization

- **Healthy:** are all five *working together?*
  - All APEST functions coming together to serve, equip, partner and build up the Body and extend the Kingdom and so working in partnership for the good of the organization
  - The culture of the organization is a healthy reflection of the strengths and participation of each of the APEST functions
  - No competing, disjointed or individualistic perspectives or agendas

- **Transforming:** are all five *accessing synergy and leveraging strengths?*
  - Leaders bringing maturity to the culture of the organization by investing, partnering and serving fruitfully alongside other APEST functions
  - Leaders engaging, training and releasing other leaders within other APEST gifting/functions as well as their own APEST base
  - Leaders seeing fruitfulness in leadership beyond their own individual competency as they are accessing other APEST functions in intentional partnership

- **Transcending:** are all five *recreating* themselves?
  - Conscious competence—leaders being self-aware about how they have grown in their fivefold ministry and intentionally training others in order to pass on wisdom and experience and grow maturity
  - Each APEST is training and apprenticing others and releasing generations of their particular calling
  - The organization expresses maturity, unity and fullness though APEST leadership expressed in culture, structure and leadership at every level.

Tactics

These tactics will give you and your team the opportunity to identify and realize 5Q potential more effectively in the people and places of your context and across your organization. We have shared some principles and perspectives on identifying and activating 5Q in parenting, the workplace, church gatherings and missional or mid-sized communities. We'd encourage you to reflect on and process these tactics together as a team to be able to see where 5Q maturity is strong or weak across your organization and context, and to learn and grow through reflective practice and experiential learning.

APEST in the Workplace: Seeing 5Q In Everyday Spaces

by Chris Harrison

Once you get familiar with the core characteristics of APEST, you begin to see them functioning all around you. Here are some pointers to help identify these 5Q personalities in the workplace, and how to apply your knowledge for maximum impact.

The Apostle in the Staff Meeting

- Whose voice is priming the organization for innovation and entrepreneurship?
- Who is developing capacities for appropriate risk taking?
- Who is challenging the room to dream dreams? To imagine the company forward?
- Who reminds the room of the greater vision and their commitment to maintain it?
- Who walks from office to office challenging and inspiring people to see themselves in new ways?

That's the Pioneer, the Innovator, the Entrepreneur, the Culture Creator at work.
There's your *Apostle.*

The Prophet in the Board Room

- Who is maintaining self-critical insight in the organization and the employees?
- Who questions policy and decisions when they become inhuman, self-protective and/or oppressive?
- Who safeguards the organization from missional drift? From straying from the vision? From wandering too far from the values that maintain the organizational integrity?
- Who confronts power when it is vital to do so?
- Who fuels passion for the company's purpose?

That's the Activist, the Intercessor, the "Passionary."
There's the *Prophet.*

The Evangelist on the Marketing Call

- Who is naturally developing an invitational and welcoming culture?
- Who develops the stickiness and simplicity of the core message?
- Who reaches out, connecting outsiders to insiders, to the product or service?
- Who maintains positive, life-affirming and redeeming "vibes" in the organization or office?
- Who consistently champions the cultural relevance of the organization?

That is the Networker, the Deal Maker, the Marketer, the Storyteller.
   There's the *Evangelist*.

The Shepherd by the Water Cooler

- Who builds relationships with the marginalized, the different, the non-performers?
- Who creates space where the hurting can feel cared for? The quieted can be heard?
- Who spends more time listening and relating than they do speaking and directing?
- Who works with employees, helping them gain experience, growing in their positions and skills?
- Who works to ensure the appropriate protection of employees and customers?

That is the Healer, the Relator, the Human Resource rep, the Community Developer.
   There's the *Shepherd*.

The Teacher at the Xerox

- Who develops resources, policies and programs for continued learning?
- Who is committed to strong means of knowledge transfer?
- Who encourages active learning experiences, perhaps through case studies, role play and new practices?
- Who works in such a way that they cultivate a culture of curiosity and love of organizational insight?
- Who creates a culture of organizational wisdom, departmental congruence and best practices?

That is the Mentor, the Educator, the Thinker/Philosopher, the Instructor.
   There's the *Teacher*.

Like a healthy church, a healthy organization will also nurture all five of the APEST roles. Granted, in most workplaces they won't perform a Christian function, but this shows that the 5Q typology is so primordial, so foundational, it can be observed everywhere.

If you are able to start identifying the 5Q qualities that you see in the people around you, you can begin to shape a 5Q team around you, a group of diverse gifting that together bring a wholeness, productivity and an energized approach to projects, meetings and everyday conversations.

If you have trouble figuring who has which particular gifting, engage people. Ask questions: Ask them about their passions. What do they love most about working where they do? Doing what they do? If they could do anything what would it be? What was their favorite job? What is their dream job? Why?

These questions will lead you in the direction of their 5Q.

Once you are dialled into the personalities around you, here are some ways to approach 5Q on the job:

> **Make sure to include all five personalities in critical conversations.**
> **Ask questions like, "What would Mike say about this?" Or, "What would Sally add if she were here?"**

How can you bring 5Q voices into discussion where they aren't usually? If you can't move people around, include different 5Q functions in your thinking:

> **"How would a *Mentor* approach working with Stan?"**
> **"Do we need the help of a *Healer/Relator* in this tense situation?"**
> **"How could a *Storyteller* improve the focus of my front office?"**
> **"What would change if an *Intercessor* spoke truth in this moment?"**
> **"Do we need an *Innovator* to help us see a way forward that we are missing?"**

APEST in Parenting: Praying the Five Modes of Christ's Presence

By Jon Ritner

After reading 5Q, I wondered if the APEST acronym would make a meaningful prayer guide. I asked a friend to create a graphic summary of the five gifts using all the synonyms and titles I found in 5Q. Then I printed one and put it in my kids' room by their beds. At night, I pray through each of the five modes of Christ's presence in my kids' lives and in the life of our family. I try to filter the events and opportunities of the week through the five functions. I am amazed how each night the Spirit leads me to specific behaviors, character qualities, and habitual practices that I want to see become evident in our life as a family. As these prayers begin to bear fruit, I believe we will become a more effective example of Jesus and the Kingdom of God to the world around us. Here is the summary sheet created by my designer friend, Kevin Miller, as well as some examples of how I have been praying.[23]

Function	Prayer
APOSTLE	"Give our family the courage to take risks rooted in the Spirit's leading. Help us to step out into adventure and liminality where real growth most often occurs." "Thank you for my daughter's bravery to try new things and may she not lose that innovative and creative passion as she enters Middle School."
PROPHET	"Help our family to see systems that need reforming in Hollywood so that we can advocate for those with less influence than us." "Grow in my son a heart that is willing to tell the truth when confronted about his behavior."
EVANGELIST	"Give us a deep love for those living around us in our apartment complex and provide space and opportunity for us to be Jesus to our neighbors through hospitality and friendship." "Help my kids to always see those on the margins, the left out, and the looked over, and let them be leaders at including them at school."
SHEPHERD	"Thank you for my son's tenderheartedness and empathy for others. Help him to know how to use that gift to serve others but also protect him from those who seek to harm him because of his generosity." "Deepen within my kids a heart to help and serve each other and their friends first before they seek their own interests."
TEACHER	"Create a passion for your Word in our life. Help us to learn and live out your truth, especially our memory verses." "Help my kids to retain their French language skills that they learned in Brussels."

Table 5.2 Example of Praying the Five Modes of Christ's Presence

APEST in Church Gatherings

With contributions from Jon Ritner, Craig Ogden, Ben Rook and Rich Robinson

Below are a few tried and test methods and testimonies from church practitioners seeking to increase the levels of APEST awareness and engagement through the gathered Sunday service, and consequently throughout the rest of the week.

66 As I teach through the gifts, we are interviewing members of the church body to ask them to discuss how that week's specific gift is lived out in their public-sector life (third place, work place, families, etc.). Letting everyday people be the heroes has been huge, as well as giving practical examples for those still learning the 5Q language. Below is an example from my teaching on the Teaching function. I talked about the general characteristics and functions of Teachers and then called out members of my congregation[24] who exemplified those characteristics. 99

Table 5.3 Exemplification of Teaching Characteristics

Characteristic of the Teaching Function	Exemplified in Congregation Member
Teachers create traditions and document memories that preserve a culture over a long period of time	Sophie Lyall creating photo books, memory boxes, birthday plates
Teachers help create policies and systems that solidify a team and give it stability as it grows	Seth Foster managing our financial stability, operating our budget
Teachers help create resources to equip others to do their jobs better	Lily Goins just published a notebook to help screenwriters arrange their story better
Teachers celebrate milestones and track progress	Beth Ford as a cell group leader, documented everyone's birthday to make sure they get celebrated in the group
Teachers organize and systematize things so that others can access them easily	Jonathan Scott wrote a whole book on how to organize and format a script, so that others can actually read it
Teachers have a contagious love for learning that inspires others to continue growing as well	Chris Spencer in our kids club—contagious energy

Characteristic of the Teaching Function	Exemplified in Congregation Member
Teachers are able to explain complex ideas and facilitate new learning experiences for others	Steve Myers in my community group integrating creation and science
Teachers are often practical, grounded, rational thinkers that offer wise advice and help maintain good decision-making processes	Emma Hill on our elders' doctrinal team, long after a meeting, still mulling over our conversations, checking it with others in our community
Teachers naturally look to mentor others and train the next generation	Lucas Dean, cell group leader, has mentored a whole generation of our current cell group leaders

(Jon Ritner, Ecclesia Hollywood)

66 We found it really important to have a teaching series that corresponds to each of the fivefold so that we could validate people with those vocations. We went through each of the fivefold, doing a Sunday teaching in the gathered setting. Members would then revisit the message in missional communities and have a number of questions they responded to.

We try to think about the sweep of the year and try to validate the fivefold from the front so that we are enabling members to all feel they have a place and to give an encouragement for everyone to serve according to their gifting.

We also interviewed people at the front asking them about their APEST vocations. One time, we interviewed a whole family who not only talked about their own personal vocation but how that affected how they interacted with each other and how they raised their family. 99

(Craig Ogden, Plentylife Church, Victoria, Australia)

66 We have been creating ministry teams, some of which are fivefold focused to speak into Missional Communities and larger gatherings. They also cross-pollinate so that the prophetic team meets with the worship team and equips them for Spirit-led worship, for example. 99

(Ben Rook, Pathway Community Church, Leicester, UK)

66 It's important to create a 'gatherings team' that represents each of the fivefold so that together they can think and plan gatherings which will incorporate and utilize the synergy and symphony of APEST. So, for example in a planning meeting, the apostle will always be reflecting on the gathered expression being a place to equip the members to be sent out. The prophet will be championing the encounter of God in worship and the space for engagement with God. The evangelist will be thinking about the non-Christians that will be attending and how the elements of the gathering are communicated effectively to them. The shepherd will be encouraging the team to reflect on how everyone is known, welcomed and connected, and the teacher will be moving the conversation toward the depth and systematic teaching and training and equipping people in God's word. All of these are vital for a mature gathering and so we need each of the fivefold voice represented as we plan in the team meeting and as we gather as the people of God. 99

(Rich Robinson, Catalyse Change)

APEST in Missional Communities

By Rich Robinson and Brandon Schaeffer

Many across the church are engaging in local contexts using missional communities or mid-sized communities (missional vision focused on a network or neighborhood, social space size—15-30 adults—and with regular rhythms of devotion, fellowship and mission). A leader, or leaders, will uniquely lead their Missional Community (MC) depending on their base-gifting (see "base and phase" in the tools section earlier in this chapter) or the APEST make-up of the leadership team. A naturally apostolic leader, for example, will start, lead, sustain and multiply a missional community *very differently* to a teacher.

Growth and maturity in a MC will happen when leaders seek the symphony and synergy of all five functions. For example, a mature and effective apostolic leader is seeking to engage and release the other four. This process may involve recruiting other leaders with particular fivefold gifts or engaging other perspectives around the fivefold. So a healthy MC will have a leading beat or primary influence from the base calling and function of the leader but should have a team and a culture that reflects a healthy distribution and expression of each of the fivefold.

How Does Each APEST Base Tend to Lead Missional Communities?

Apostle-led Missional Community :>

These will usually be dynamic and engaging, orbiting around someone who overflows with charisma and possesses the ability to inspire and gather others. Frequently their groups will grow quickly, and multiplication is on the agenda from the start. This rapid growth and agenda of multiplication is because of the apostle's focus on sentness but can produce pressure on the group due to the speed of growth. A mature apostle must have the skills to manage such a maneuver and the relational implications that it brings.

Prophet-led Missional Community ▽

This community will tend to focus on the mission, but will not be as evangelistic. They are often highly visible, since they desire an incarnational approach to presenting the Gospel. Generally this means their groups are very radical, with the highest of demands placed upon members. If you have ever encountered a group whose talk—and subsequent action—focuses on reclaiming their city by their very presence and engagement with the people out on the streets, then it is probably a group with strong prophetic leadership. Such groups *can* grow by multiplying, but often they will keep the core team and allow a new work to bud off into a new context.

Evangelist-led Missional Community ◁:

The goal is to go straight after the People of Peace (Luke 10) in their chosen mission context. Evangelism is top of the agenda (unsurprisingly!). They will identify the gatekeepers in the community, engage intentionally and relationally and then stay with them. Often you see evangelists going out in pairs, finding a few People of Peace, building relationships. They desire to win an entire unreached neighborhood through these relationships. These MCs usually have a high number of non-Christians within the relational orbit.

Shepherd-led Missional Community :O:

Shepherds long to bring community transformation by establishing and then building on long-term relationships. They value the integrity of becoming embedded in their context. This means while things are not as spectacular at first, they have a slower and long-lasting approach to mission. This model often works well in the suburbs. Relationships are at the heart of everything shepherds do, so it can be more difficult for them to multiply. They will generally tend to prioritize depth over breadth. They find it easier to grow as an offshoot—a small group of people who take what they are doing into a neighboring area.

Teacher-led Missional Community ˙ö˙

Teachers will frequently give of themselves to model how to live the Christian life—whether in worship, community or mission. Mature teachers will do so humbly. It won't even feel like they are teaching much of the time but there will always be an instructing, training and coaching element to their leadership and community life. They will tend to commit for a long season, but many will eventually begin to seek a fresh context requiring their help and then release their group to a strong manager. They will send out new groups who will be characterized by having been thoroughly prepared with a clear model of how to do things.

Identifying APEST Growth for your Group or Organization

By Rich Robinson

As leaders, we're often asking questions, trying to analyze what's missing and why. The questions below are intended for small groups, missional communities, churches or organizations who identify a deficit in their leadership culture or practice. Using the questions helps to identify which of the fivefold the deficit relates to and therefore where the need is for coaching or additional input.[25] This is a good resource for leaders within your wider organization who may not be taking the full test but can use this to analyze their current leadership and practice.

Apostle ∴>

- We feel like we need a jolt, things are too settled and stale. How do I mix things up?
- We feel we need some fresh perspective. How do I have some outside eyes and wisdom for a fresh push or start?
- We feel like we are missing opportunities and not realizing all the potential within the community. How do I make the most of those in my community?
- We feel we are stuck in the present. How do we know how to get moving again?
- We are unsure as leaders/as a community of the way ahead. How do we work out which way to go and the direction to pursue?
- We are not growing in number or making progress forward; all we are doing is managing people and organizing events. How do we re-cast vision, kick-start the process and get us moving forward again?

Prophet ⬇

- We need clarity on God's word for us as leaders or as a community. How do we go about discerning this?
- We know we need more depth, a stronger culture and more integrity. Where do we start and how do we grow deeper as Christians and as community?
- We want everyone in the community to grow in hearing God and responding to what he is saying. How do we help them?
- We feel unsure of the way ahead and want God to speak into this? How do we as a leadership team hear God well together?
- We feel like people are just responding to culture and environment. How do we help them live wholeheartedly and passionately for Jesus in a countercultural way?

Evangelist 📢

- We are disconnected from the local community. How do we go about connecting with people in a real way?
- We feel we have a "church life" and a "work" or "family" life? How do we live one life and share our faith authentically?
- We have people who are not at all confident in their faith and in sharing their faith. How do we grow a confidence in the gospel and in sharing the gospel?
- We have lots of opportunities with People of Peace, but we're not sure how to take them further or what to say. How do we move forward and start engaging the People of Peace to a deeper level?
- We feel like the community has become a little introspective and we are just managing Christians and organizing events. How do we engage people to have a vision and passion for the lost?

Shepherd ⦿

- We feel like there is a lack of depth of love, care and relationships in the community. How do we start to help people engage with each other deeply?
- We feel the community is quite closed. How do we envision people to welcome and love the stranger and outsider?
- We feel the community is slightly fragmented and feels individualistic. How do we help people love sacrificially and intentionally?

- We feel like we do all the helping, caring and loving as a leadership team. How do we equip the community to look after each other, not just rely on the leadership?
- We feel we are not loving People of Peace and non-Christians well. How do we help our community to love well and in doing so model Jesus to people?

Teacher

- We feel like there is an immaturity in handling God's word. How do we help people to mature in their knowledge and application of the Bible?
- We feel people are unsure of how to share their faith because of arguments or opposition. How do we equip the community to be mature and confident in their biblical foundations?
- We feel that the community depend on us as a leadership to share what we think from our reading of Scripture. How do we equip every member of the community to feed themselves from Scripture?
- We feel people are discipled by peers, TV, social media and their own brokenness. How do we help our community engage with God's truth to grow in their identity as a disciple?
- We feel we don't know where to start on people developing patterns of word, worship and prayer. Where do we start and how do we start?

NOTES

Key Headlines to Reflect On

Key Discussion Topics to Process

Key Action Points for Next Steps

SECTION THREE

EXPLORE
(THE JOURNEY)

6

Notes for the Journey Ahead

We hope this short section will prepare you for the journey towards maturity, so that as you begin to implement the tools and tactics from the previous section you're not thwarted by an unexpected bump in the road, or discouraged by what appears to be regression. We all know from our experience of life that growth is never straightforward or in a straight line. Life and learning does not happen in a linear or incremental fashion. Our aim is for the maturity that Paul sets out in Ephesians 4, and in an ever-increasing individualistic society we need to be reminded that the process of maturity does not happen in a vacuum.

The journey toward greater APEST maturity for you as a team will involve *integration* and *iteration*. We need to appreciate the value of one another (integration), and we need to learn and persevere through the ups and downs we experience (iteration). Anyone who has downloaded a recipe off the internet, tried to learn a language, or has read every parenting book out there, knows that even if we have all the information at our fingertips, living it out and putting it into practice is a completely different ball game. To learn a language or to parent in isolation means that our growth is stunted—we see things from our limited perspective and we don't utilize the skills, gifts and experience of others to aid our growth.

The Way We Grow

Most people and organizations think of growth in terms of ladders. There is one rung—you climb it, stand on it, learn it, and then you move on up to the next rung. But this is not how *anything* develops in the natural world. It is not how a forest grows, how your body grows, or even how your understanding grows.

Figure 6.1 Perceived Path of Maturity

There are no linear ladders in the natural world or in organic systems. Rather, there are webs that together create a system.

Webs are the patterns of networks. A forest is a network of trees, and it grows in this way. Your body is a network of cells, called organs, which are also networked. Everything operates in relationship to one another.

This "web of skills" is as true for the organization as it is for the individual. People have to learn to work together to form a single team. Then teams or departments have to learn how to work together. There are a lot of ideas, motivations, relationships, and moving parts in that whole system. Disharmony anywhere can affect the harmony of the whole.

Now **think about this in terms of APEST**. If one APEST function is not present, or not meaningfully integrated into the whole, the organization is *limited* in its strength and it cannot get any stronger than it already is. When this happens, it means that the wisdom, experience, and passion of that capacity is cut off. The community is not given the chance to learn from it and to grow.

If one function is not integrated, it's as if it were not present at all—growth and maturity are limited. This is how the integration of the different APEST capacities literally helps the whole organization to mature. The degree of that integration also indicates the degree of maturity.

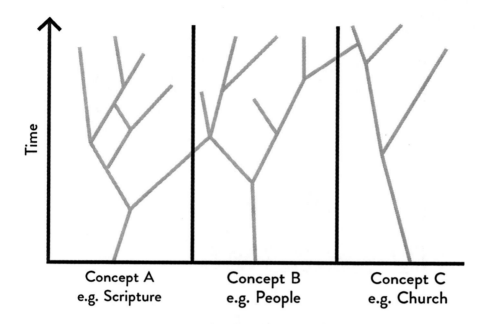

Figure 6.2 Actual Path of Maturity: An interpretation of Kurt Fischer and Todd Rose's (2001) Web of Skills, as cited in Schenck, 2011[26]

Development = Growth *and* Regression

There are times when the webs are growing rapidly. It's like a coin drops in the slot, everything falls into place and it all makes sense. The one thing we understand opens up a whole new realm of possibilities. One small thing can make a huge difference. And there are other times when we feel stuck, staring at the same situation unsure of how to learn or grow or get past it. This usually happens when the whole web is waiting on one part to catch up and integrate. Once the lagging area catches up and connects, a whole new set of possibilities open up, and rapid growth continues. Because webs are interconnected systems, when something new integrates into the system, it literally changes the entire web.

Teams or departments need to connect in new ways and learn from one another. But there is a timeline and process to this dynamic: It takes time for people to learn how to work with one another in new ways, to learn what one team's perspective means for the work another team is doing. It is because of this fact that the speed of growth, change, and integration over time takes the form of an s-shaped curve.[27]

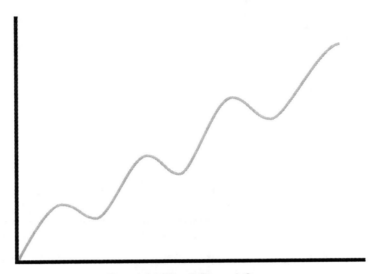

Figure 6.3 The S-Shaped Curve

In terms of APEST maturity, the s-shaped curve (of growth and stall) is the shape of growth for both the whole organization and for each individual area. We don't naturally grow in a linear fashion. Natural development includes both growth and regression, moving at an uneven pace. It is unrealistic to expect that a person will grow in their understanding or expression of any single APEST capacity at a steady rate, and the same is true for the integration of the different APEST capacities within an organization.

It's important to understand this for two reasons:

Firstly, the peaks of growth are exciting; you begin to work things out and get in a groove. Things are clicking, and goals are being reached. These are pleasant spaces that we want to stay in for a long time. But they can become spaces that trap us. In growth and development, there really are no plateaus. Plateaus are just what you experience before change happens and you go into a valley. There is no flattening out and coasting into the future on past success. The rule seems to be written into the nature of many things. S-curve shaped growth is inevitable.

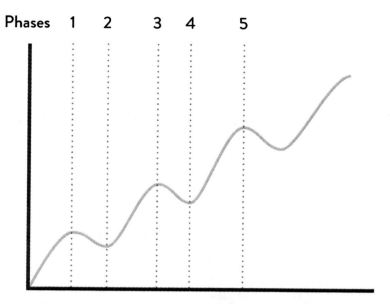

Figure 6.4 The S-Shaped Curve and Corresponding Phases

Secondly, we hope that the s-shaped curve of growth and maturation will encourage you when you hit walls, tensions, and places where it may feel like you are moving backwards. That is what valleys feel like. Change can be hard, scary, and painful. But be greatly encouraged: If you don't give up and press forward to learn more about why things are not working, the journey itself will move you through the valley and into a new space of integration and maturity!

Putting the Journey Together

As we have already noted, in growth and development **all things are interrelated.** We must move toward integration, resisting our culture of individualism and our compartmentalized mindset. One aspect of APEST can only *be fully understood* in its complete integration with the others. That is why Jesus is the model and the standard. He is the perfect example of each APEST capacity, and *perfection can only exist if it is integrated into one entity.* And because of this, a full understanding and mature expression of the APEST functions can only happen in the *organization*—in a *group* of mutually committed people.

Just as a symphony or a jazz quartet collaborate to create an emergent sound, so too the various parts of Jesus' Body create a super-abundant form of synergy. Synergy involves the interaction or cooperation of two or more agents in a system to produce a combined effect greater than the sum of their separate effects. In the math of the Body it means that 1 + 1 + 1 = 5 or more. Jesus has intended that we are better and more effective together than we can ever be apart—that is why we are called to strive to maintain our God-given unity. We simply cannot do it alone, nor are we meant to. *We need to become a living web, living stones, teaching and learning from one another.*

An organization needs all functions of the APEST to reach the standard Jesus set for the church, and the process of doing that is called development and maturation. This is a *collective* responsibility. It is not merely the responsibility of professional clergy or elite title holders. It is the responsibility of *all* believers.

It is the organization's responsibility, therefore, to disciple and grow people in the redeemed and reformed APEST capacities by integrating their individual gifts into the group and expressing the functions of APEST as a collective. What a beautiful expression of the Body of Christ and what a brilliant ecology God designed to cultivate us!

Visualizing Maturity—The Cone-Shape of Development

Throughout this book, we've contended for a holistic, healthy church that is actively expressing all of the functions of the APEST capacities. In such a church, the APEST functions are of equal value and importance for the overall function, health and witness of the church. If any one area is missing, it creates an asymmetrical, imbalanced witness of Jesus.

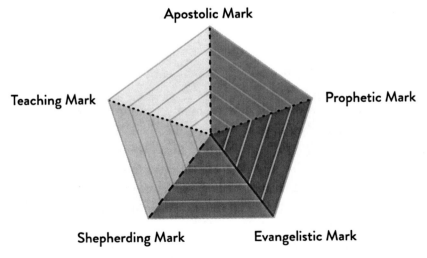

Figure 6.5 APEST Functions of the Organization

What might full maturity in the Body of Christ look like? What should we be aiming at through our corporate, ecclesial life as the distinctly Jesus-shaped people we are called to be? Although developing a personal vocational APEST profile to pursue our calling individually is important, we need to understand how the giftings actually function *corporately* for greater maturity.

The journey of APEST maturity combines what we've learnt so far: the power of integration (webs) and the path of growth (s-shaped curve). We're going to use the imagery of a cone to consider the journey of maturity. Imagine a child's ice cream cone, the embarrassing party hat you're forced to wear at Christmas or a traffic cone at the side of the road. If you think about figure 6.5 as a top-down view of a cone, then from the side (laid flat) the journey to maturity would look something like this:

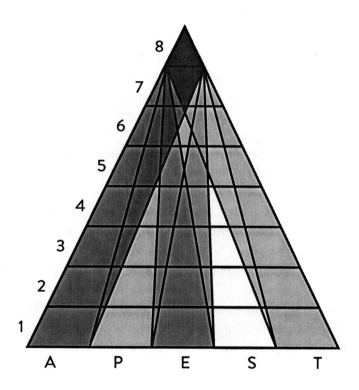

Figure 6.6 Full APEST Maturity within an Organization

As you can see, with increasing maturity (further up the cone) the APEST capacities increasingly blend. As an individual moves up the cone, their APEST capacities begin to be informed and enhanced by the APEST capacities of others. This kind of harmony is only possible in community, where all the APEST capacities are represented through the leadership team and are subsequently equipped into the body of believers. When a leadership team begin to work together in harmony, an organization will begin to function in all the APEST capacities.

The places where the colors blend and overlap are the places of revelation and maturity where different APEST functions are working together effectively. Jesus, at the top, is the fullness of all the colors. If we were looking at light, Jesus would be the full spectrum, creating white light.

Now consider an organization primarily functioning in the evangelistic but functioning at a low level in the prophetic. Such an organization is limited in how much it can mature as a whole because it is deficient in at least one of the five marks, and consequently doesn't bear much resemblance to the fullness of Jesus.

At some point, the evangelistic function will need the prophetic to be able to mature in itself. For example, the prophetic can help the evangelistic function to listen and look for where God is at work in people or places. *Without the complementary understandings of the other APEST capacities, the growth of each isolated APEST is stunted and will likely hit its ceiling at around phase three.* Sadly, this probably describes the vast majority of Protestant churches in the Western cultural context, most of which have reached a ceiling at the phase of their own siloed APEST capacity. Without the understanding and practice of APEST, a church or organization can never mature towards the fullness of Christ outlined in Ephesians 4 and it therefore remains dysfunctional and immature. We've already noted that we live in a culture that over-emphasizes independence, self-improvement and solo-heroes, and we can't overestimate the impact that has on our ability to build collaborative and interdependent leadership teams. It's countercultural for us to think collaboratively, and it's one of the key reasons why high-impact missional movements are so incredibly rare in Western contexts.

We were created to be a Body that reflects one hero—Jesus. To reach the higher phases of maturity (3+) each of the individual APEST streams needs to learn to deeply value the full expression of each of the others. Competency and maturity cannot exist without significant cross-fertilization and integration of all of the five functions. An organization is not truly competent in any one function if it does not have at least some degree of integration with each of the other APEST functions.

A Note on Competency *and* Character

If we are truly to pattern ourselves after Jesus, it involves imitating both the character and competency of Jesus. Jesus calls us to follow him—to be his disciples—which means we are to learn to love as he loves (**character**) and do as he did (**competency**). When we apply this to growing in APEST, it means that we are to grow in the *skills* of the fivefold as Jesus demonstrated but also to operate in them with the *character* of Jesus. A mature teacher, for example, isn't just skilled at training and equipping others in God's word (**competency**). She has also learned how to love people where they are at, speaking to them in humility and kindness, and being compelled to see each of them walk in the call of God on their life (**character**). We are empowered to live this through the Holy Spirit. As we abide in Christ (John 15), we increasingly reflect him and exude the fruits of the Spirit (Galatians 5).

Going at the Right Pace

It is also worth considering the *pace* of growth. We live in a fast-paced instant society. And as disciples of Jesus, it's easy to absorb that culture and become overambitious about growth and development, trying to speed up the process or even skip or jump phases. We read a book like this one and want to go full steam ahead! But Jesus calls us to be at rest in the process, for his yoke is easy and his burden is light (see Matthew 11:28–30).

After decades of facilitating growth and development, I (Jessie) have learned two key things. First, *the pace of development belongs to God.* He is in charge of the growth (1 Corinthians 3:6–7), he is "author and finisher of our faith" (Hebrews 12:2, KJV), and he is sovereign. If he chooses to accelerate growth, to God be the glory. If he chooses to slow down, to God be the glory. We are simply responsible for our obedience. God knows what he is doing, and we have to trust him with each other and the church.

The second thing is that *we shouldn't skip ahead.* If we attempt to skip the process, personal character is often sacrificed. As Romans 5 says, character is built in a person through suffering (pain) and perseverance (time). Talent may get you title or position, but we need to grow in character if we are to imitate Christ and if we are to lead and equip others in his ways and works.

It is often said that we are educated far beyond our capacity for obedience. It's no use shouting louder and being more passionate if most people never put our sermons into practice. Discipleship is of vital and strategic importance because it encourages individuals to grow in the ways, words, and works of Jesus which, as we have already noted, involves growth in both character **and** competency, rather than simply absorbing more *information.*

STOP

Awareness

Thinking about growing in APEST maturity:

Where do you need to be at rest?

Where do you need to trust?

Where are you rushing ahead?

Where do you need to be more proactive and move forward?

Application

In your particular calling, commit to a process to grow in the character and competency of Jesus. Identify two next steps in both areas and a person to hold you accountable.

NOTES

Key Headlines to Reflect On

Key Discussion Topics to Process

Key Action Points for Next Steps

7

Where to from Here

The 5Q Collective (*www.5Qcentral.com*)

We are aware that transformation doesn't just happen through learning new paradigms and information.

We would like to share with you the opportunity to engage further on a transformative journey that will involve deepening your own discipleship and strengthening your leadership, as well developing the capacities of your church or organization.

Our coaching and training aims to create a process where theological imagination and innovative practice in discipleship, leadership and mission can be engaged and activated throughout the Body of Christ.

Our training will begin by developing competencies in 5Q generally and then going on to develop competency in all five capacities or quotients individually. We call these focused streams AQ (apostolic quotient), PQ (prophetic quotient), and EQ (evangelistic quotient), and so on. We are currently focused on getting a full AQ training system up and running within a year. We will then start working on developing the coaching and training for PQ, EQ, SQ and TQ—so keep your eyes out for that in the future.

These various coaching and training processes provide strategic, practical, training for transformative discipleship practice, leadership development, and organizational change.

There are shorter and longer-term ways to engage in learning. These processes include:

5Q System Training

5Q Competency Coaching (14 weeks)

5Q Coaching cohorts provide an environment and experience which provides an initial look at the core content, key principles and personal practices for 5Q as a whole. There is opportunity for peer engagement, reflective learning, deeper study, as well as coaching from seasoned APEST practitioners. These cohorts can be for individual leaders wanting to grow in understanding and application of 5Q or for a church/organization wanting to take intentional steps into greater understanding and application of 5Q.

5Q Leadership Cohorts (14 months)

Leadership cohorts will be the peak training experience offered. In this training, we will focus on grasping the sheer potency of 5Q thinking, becoming competent in practicing APEST dynamics, and learning how to create an authentic 5Q culture in a given organization. 5Q Leadership cohorts are communities of leaders or leadership teams coming together regionally as well as online on a regular basis.

The online and on-the-ground leadership cohort experience is designed to provide a forum for best thinking and best practices for teams to engage with the 5Q content in a deeper way through individual learning, group discussion, and coaching and training in the use of various tools.

This will be an amazing learning journey for individual leaders as well as teams.

Specialty Tracks (AQ, PQ, EQ, SQ, TQ)

AQ Competency Coaching (14 weeks)

Coaching cohorts provide an environment and experience which will delve deeper into the key principles and personal practices for developing apostolic ministry and leadership (AQ). There is the opportunity for peer engagement, reflective learning and further study, input and coaching. These coaching cohorts can be for individual leaders wanting to grow in engagement and practice of apostolic or prophetic leadership or for a church/organization wanting to take intentional steps into greater understanding and application of AQ.

AQ Leadership Cohorts (14 months)

Leadership cohorts are the peak training experience that we will offer, and we believe are entirely unique in that they provide a forum for the development of the apostolic gift in our time. AQ Leadership cohorts will come together regionally, as well as online, on a regular basis. Our aim is to create a rich relational environment, offer high-level training enfolded in a best-practices educational process. Our ultimate aim to is to create a burgeoning global network of apostolic practitioners who will pioneer new territories and chart the maps for others to follow.

The online and on-the-ground leadership cohort experience is designed to provide a forum for best thinking and best practices for apostolic practitioners that have both a self-identified, and a collectively confirmed, call to apostolic ministry as well as a proven track record.

It's our belief that identifying, developing, and networking apostolic leaders is a crucial factor in catalyzing transformative missional movements around the world.

PQ and EQ – Coaching cohorts and leadership cohorts

We are developing an accessible and replicable training system upon the missional paradigm of APEST which will serve to equip and empower prophets and evangelists as well as those wanting to receive training in the prophetic and evangelistic functions. There will be both coaching cohorts and leadership cohorts available moving forward.

Tests (www.5qcentral.com/tests/)

The 5Q Diagnostic Test

This is designed to give a **snapshot** of your organization's current **expression** of the fivefold intelligences.

The 5Q Systems Analysis Test

This is a more advanced test that measures the levels of organizational awareness and maturity in APEST thinking.

Both of these tests can be found at www.5qcentral.com/tests/ and are explored in more detail in the appendix.

Blog (www.5qcentral.com/blog/)

The blog is regularly updated with 5Q content from practitioners around the globe on various topics. It's a wealth of information and experience to aid you on the journey.

Conclusion

What Does It Take to Make Disciples Of All Nations?

What does it take to make disciples of all nations? This is our call, our mandate, our commission from Jesus himself. In truth, we may not understand the depth and complexity of the task. The disciples certainly didn't—they did not even know about the North American, South American or Australian continents.

Though we may not understand, Jesus certainly did. He not only understood what it means to make disciples of all nations, he also empowered and released us to do it. He promised that he would be with us, and while that is true in so many exciting and amazing ways, it is also true that he is with us in the APEST gifts.

But here is what we believe. Here is our strong conviction. We believe that it will take *all five* of the gifts of Jesus to the church—the apostolic, the prophetic, the evangelistic, the shepherding, and the teaching capacities—operating in their fullness in the Body of Christ, to carry out our mandate. We need the APEST to fulfill the Great Commission and command of Jesus.

But who Jesus calls, he also equips (Hebrews 13:21). He has called all of us and equipped all of us as a collective Body to fulfill this mandate. We hope and pray that as the church embraces the gifts of Jesus and begins to intentionally grow in the APEST functions in society, that the Great Commission will seem less overwhelming and more within our reach. It requires Jesus in us and through us, and he would not have it any other way.

Appendix

Evaluating Your Organization with the 5Q Tests

We have developed two specific tests to help churches and organizations accurately measure their current expression of APEST as well as assess their depth of awareness, understanding, and application of it throughout the organization. These can be purchased at www.5qcentral.com/tests/. This appendix explores the tests in more detail, as well as providing suggestions for actionable next steps.

During the twentieth century it was discovered, in both science and psychology, that the simple act of measuring something changes it. Someone asks you where your big toe is *right now*; you wiggle it to identify where it is. But you have moved it in order to locate it, and that process moves it from where it was when the question was asked. If the question had not been asked, you would not have moved your toe. The act of trying to measure something inherently changes it.

Think about it in relation to the 5Q Diagnostic and 5Q Systems Analysis tests. There are people who are interested in taking this assessment—you, perhaps. That means you are already primed about getting the results, interested in what they mean. Will they confirm what you already know? Will they show you something new? What will you do with what you learn from them? You have already changed simply because you have engaged in the journey this far. Even if this is the only section you read, you are already changed by it!

Assessing APEST as an Organization

Think for a moment about going to the doctor for an annual check-up. The goal is to check your overall health and see if anything detectable has developed in the last year. But what if, instead of taking and testing your blood to check your current liver functions, they used outpatient surgery to remove part of your liver, put it in a petri dish, and tested it to see how it was functioning. That does not seem to make a lot of sense, right? Because the goal of the medical assessment is not how your liver cells function in isolation, but rather how your organ is functioning *in the organism*.

You cannot test the health or vitality of an organism (or organization) by testing components in isolation from the system. Such an assessment is not authentic—it won't give you an accurate picture. Authentic assessment only happens when things are measured in *relation* to and in the *context* of their environment. Parts can be looked at individually, but not in isolation. And the person conducting the assessment always knows that the whole organism is greater than the sum of its parts.

Take, for example, the liver illustration. Perhaps you are ill, but your liver is functioning just fine. Looking at your liver cells in isolation reveals that they are healthy and working. If this were your only assessment, you would never discover that while the liver is fine, the ducts that connect the liver to the small intestine have blockages, and thus the enzymes the liver makes are not getting to the rest of the body. You would only know this by examining the whole organism.

In this example, the issue is the *connection* between two organs. Connection points are often where breakdowns in organizations occur, keeping them from operating in a healthy way. It is usually not any one person or any one team that is causing the "sickness," but something that happens in the dynamic *interaction* between people and departments. This is why a holistic assessment is needed, so that the results can be authentic and the assessment can be both meaningful and actionable.[28]

Who Takes the Tests?

Because we are assessing an **organization**, both the 5Q Diagnostic and 5Q Systems Analysis tests are to be taken by a **group** and not in isolation. It is best if they are taken by the leadership team in a church, whether a person is paid, full-time, licensed, lay leader, or elder. If a person is an influencer in the direction of the church and has some level of authority to execute, then they should be part of the group taking the assessment. If you have more than ten people in your leadership team whom you would like to take the assessment, then they should take the assessment as departments, councils, teams, or other naturally occurring groups.

Guidelines for Using the Tests

We suggest that users who are just beginning to engage with APEST start with the personal APEST Vocational Profile (either the personal profile or the more comprehensive 360-degree profile—both of which can be accessed at www.5qcentral.com/tests). This will allow users to see how the fivefold typology of ministry impacts all of God's people.

Leaders should start with the straightforward **5Q Diagnostic Test** and supplement this with insights from the personal APEST profiles of various people in the community/team. Then once the ideas and the language takes root, and awareness and practice develops, the organization can advance to the more comprehensive **5Q Systems Test** which will provide a much greater depth of analysis.

Preparation for the Tests

Because the tests seek to analyze organizational functionality as well as personal capacity, participants at every level *ought to have some awareness of the concepts involved* as well as some *basic working definitions regarding the distinctive aspects of each APEST function.* Never presume that people understand what is meant by these functions and callings. While all participants should have commonly agreed-upon working definitions (for a quick refresh, refer to the definitions on page 3), church leadership should have significantly more understanding about both the language and the key concepts. For this reason, we *strongly* advise that the key leaders consider reading *5Q* (available to buy at www.5qcentral.com) and/or *The Permanent Revolution*[29] to ensure biblical accuracy of understanding, interpretation, and process.

Interpreting the Test Results

We will give specific guidelines for interpreting each of the tests, but it's important to note at this point that one of the key factors in the usability of any test is understanding what the results mean, as well as what they don't mean. God created us all with different strengths and weaknesses. While it is okay to have weaknesses, it is not okay for us to be alone in our weakness. We need community for us to be "whole." Thus, the results of the assessments need to be interpreted as a profile of the *community.*

The scores will be presented both individually and in aggregation and so there is therefore an *individual* assessment component to it, as well as a *group* component. This means that a level of vulnerability will be required from each person taking the test. Strong emotional leadership is required when interpreting the results to help the group analyze and discuss them in the most constructive manner possible. Leaders should also steer participants away from interpreting scores as value judgments. The scores do not indicate all an individual has to offer, what their value is to the group, or put a ceiling on their development. Just as Jesus partners with us in our limitations and weaknesses, so we are called to partner with one another as the Spirit leads.

Explanation of the 5Q Diagnostic Test

Purpose

The 5Q Diagnostic is designed to give a **snapshot** of your organization's **expression** of the fivefold intelligences. It aims to help you see what is currently active or present in your organization.

Process

Each team member fills out the questionnaire honestly and to the best of their abilities, rating how much they think the organization expresses each of the capacities. It is important not to stretch the answers in an aspirational way. The diagnostic test, like all assessments, seeks to assess and compare *actual* levels of awareness and practice within the group. The final results will be the combination of those ratings to give an overall picture. A table of each person's individual ratings is also provided for greater analysis. This is valuable for creating conversation around why people answered as they did and discussing different perceptions.

We recommend taking this assessment every one to two years.

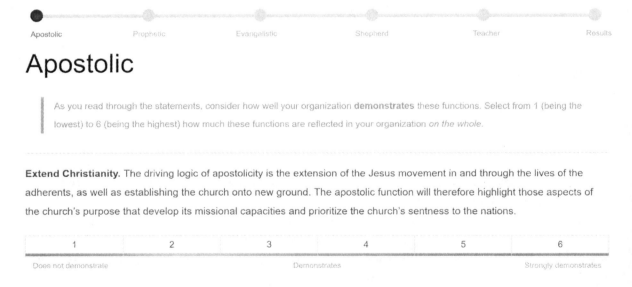

Figure A.1 Snapshot of 5Q Diagnostic Test Questionnaire

Interpreting 5Q Diagnostic Results

The test will give each group a graph indicating how individuals scored as well as a graph with an aggregated score. There is also a report that can be downloaded that will offer some strategic and tactical suggestions of how you might look at developing 5Q throughout the organization you lead. You can also use the many tools and tactics that are listed earlier in this book. We also suggest that you consider getting coaching from the 5Q Collective.[30]

In the first results chart you will see the individual scores each person gave the organization. A sample chart is depicted below.

5Q Diagnostic Individual Scores

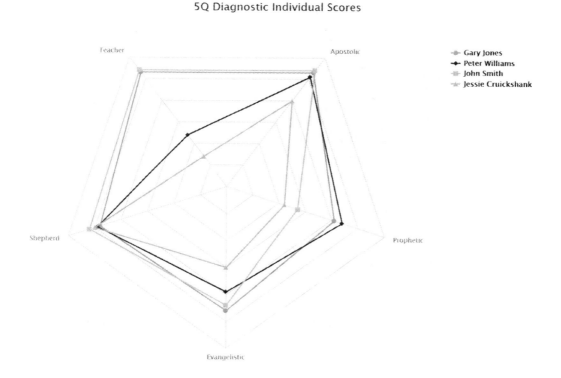

Figure A.2 5Q Diagnostic Individual Scores

The second chart on the 5Q Diagnostic's results page is the aggregated score for the organization. This will change as people complete the assessment. A sample graph is depicted below.

5Q Diagnostic Organizational Aggregate Score

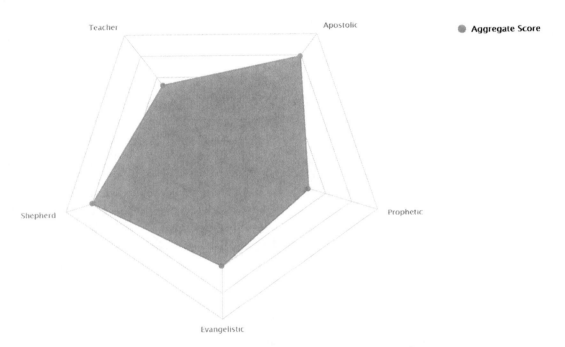

Figure A.3 5Q Diagnostic Organizational Aggregate Score

This is a 2-dimensional diagnostic assessment for those organizations who are in the early stages of implementing APEST into their organizational culture.

Explanation of the 5Q Systems Analysis

Purpose

The 5Q Systems Analysis is a more advanced test that measures the levels of organizational awareness and maturity in APEST thinking. Built on the framework of stages of maturity and learning (see "The Seven Phases of Growth" below), it not only assesses the active presence of 5Q in the church, as the straightforward diagnostic does, but also the depth of awareness, understanding, and application of it throughout the organization.

We recommend taking the 5Q Systems Analysis assessment every two or three years.

Process

The 5Q Systems Analysis looks at each team member's understanding and the overall organizational behavior across a developmental range. It measures how much a person understands about fifteen specific APEST functions. We have chosen three core functions for each APEST capacity, which means that there are three functions for the A, three for the P, etc.

SORT TASK 3

Teaching organizational function of creating a culture of accuracy and insight on theology and related disciplines

A. In a teaching organization we learn what Christianity is about as our pastor teaches what the Word of God says.

B. A teaching organization helps you better understand what you believe. It helps you ask questions and shows you how to find answers. It also helps you explain what you believe to another person by using the Bible.

C. A teaching organization understands that Truth is a person. Jesus takes ownership of stewarding truth, and reveals himself to whomever he chooses. The community has learned to open the boxes of their theology and embrace the mystery of God.

Figure A.4 Sort Task Example—5Q Systems Analysis Test

It is important to note that the 5Q Systems Analysis assessment is NOT a measure of your personal passion or calling in the APEST functions. In fact, it will look different to your personal profile. This is because the two assessments measure two different things:

The APEST Vocational Profile measures what you are drawn towards, what you value, and how you look at the world.

The Systems Test measures the *organizational* expression of APEST.

They are distinct concepts. Thinking about how we do something as a group is very different from thinking about how we do something individually. Because of the difference between individual expression of APEST and organizational expression of APEST, it should not be assumed that strong understanding in one will equate to a strong understanding in the other. The 5Q Systems Analysis test measures how much you understand of each of the functions. While how you view the world and what you value does not easily change, much of what you understand can. That is why it is important to remember that the 5Q Systems Analysis test is NOT a measure of intelligence, or what you are *capable* of understanding about the APEST functions. Rather, it is a measurement of *current* understanding which is, or course, changeable.

The Seven Phases of Growth

In our research for developing the Systems Analysis test, we were able to analyze different phases of understanding and corresponding behaviour.

There are seven phases presented in the test results.

- **Phase 1—Latent:** barely thought about, not on the radar
- **Phase 2—Opening:** beginning to develop the capacity by asking questions and wanting to know more about it
- **Phase 3—Emerging:** beginning to understand parts of it, better understanding of some parts than of others
- **Phase 4—Integrating:** parts are starting to get better, working through the hard spaces of integrating with one another
- **Phase 5—Healthy:** capacity is working well with the other capacities, in a healthy way, demonstrating general health and good understanding in this area
- **Phase 6 – Transforming:** other capacities are working together in way that is greater than the sum of its parts, in which the functions transform one another into something more
- **Phase 7 – Transcending:** rarely attained, this phase is a reminder that when we pray "on earth as it is in heaven" it can actually happen in reality.

Assessing phases gives us a three-dimensional view of an organization. Collecting data and analyzing it in this way gives us much more information than a simple profile of strengths and weaknesses. How strong is the strength? How weak is the weakness? Assessing those aspects helps the group or organization better understand where they are and better diagnose what to do next. It helps the group with setting goals in specific areas. It makes the assessment authentic and actionable.

Incidentally, there is no phase 0 church. If we followed the logic of the fivefold marks of the church, we would have to say that if a church or Christian organization did not have some degree of functionality in at least one or two of the APEST functions, it could not be considered to be a viable expression of the Body of Christ. Even an embryonic church plant or a dead congregation ought to have something to do other than simply meet together. If there was literally no mission, obedience, evangelism, pastoral care, or teaching, then while it might be considered something else, it ought not to be considered a church of Jesus Christ.

Similarly, we do not think that a phase 0 is possible in individual assessment. We believe God has written APEST into creation and thus it is in us, even in our very DNA. While capacities may be inactive or unexplored, we believe them to be present in a latent manner.

Interpreting 5Q Systems Analysis Results

The assessment results for the 5Q Systems Analysis are displayed in several tables and diagrams. First, the individual average scores for the sort analysis are given in a table and graphed (*Organizational Leadership Profile*). The second table and graph is organizational functionality results (*Organizational Functionality Profile*). The table displays the scores each individual gave the organization, while the graph layers them all together. You can turn the displayed results on and off to see how different layers of the organization (elders, staff, congregational leaders) scored the organization. The third graph is the capacity comparison (*Organizational Profile Comparison—capacity vs. execution*) which compares the best scores from the leadership profile with the average scores from the organizational functionality assessment.

1. Organizational Leadership Profile

The leadership profile maps out all of the responses of each participant's assessment on the same graph. The scores of each person, from 1 to 8, in each of the APEST areas are laid on top of one another to make a radar graph plot. Each person is identified individually, but the scores are meant to be viewed collectively.

Leadership Profile

Name	Apostolic	Prophetic	Evangelistic	Shepherding	Teaching
Orest Test	4.50	1.16	0.66	7.00	6.00
Peter Williams	6.50	1.16	8.00	0.33	7.66
Admin Admin	7.00	6.50	5.50	7.66	8.00
John Smith	6.50	5.83	3.83	5.00	5.80
Gary Jones	4.00	3.00	2.50	3.50	4.00
Orest Hrapko	4.50	5.00	4.50	4.50	3.50

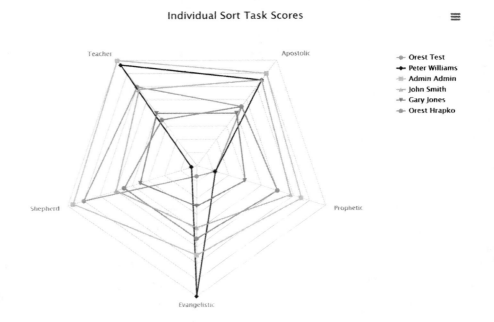

Figure A.5 Example Organizational Leadership Profile of Church A

The graph depicts the **APEST capacities inherent in the leadership team.** As you can see in the chart above, there is at least one individual who scored high in the areas of the teaching, evangelistic, and shepherding capacities. The apostolic and prophetic capacities of the leadership team are lower than the other two, in varying degrees. As a leadership team, there will be capacities the group is strong in and capacities the group is weaker in. While this is also true for individuals, the diversity of the group should mean that the group score is more balanced and symmetrical than any individual person's score.

2. Organizational Functionality Profile

The second results graph is the organizational functionality profile. This chart depicts each person's scoring of the **organization behaviors** or **performance**. This is meant to stimulate in-depth conversations regarding the profile comparison graph.

Functionality Profile

Name	Apostolic	Prophetic	Evangelistic	Shepherding	Teaching
Orest Test	3.00	4.00	6.00	8.00	6.00
Peter Williams	6.00	6.00	7.00	1.00	7.00
Admin Admin	5.00	4.00	2.00	4.00	2.00
John Smith	2.00	1.00	5.00	5.00	7.00
Gary Jones	6.00	2.00	5.50	3.50	4.00
Orest Hrapko	4.00	5.00	6.00	6.00	1.00

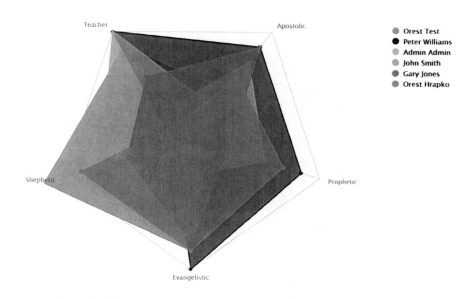

Individual Organizational Behavior Scores

Orest Test
Peter Williams
Admin Admin
John Smith
Gary Jones
Orest Hrapko

Figure A.6 Organizational Functionality Profile Results

Some leaders work with different services, or minister to different populations within the church. They may score the organization based on what they see or hear in their context, which may differ from another service or population. These varying views highlight another version of asymmetry that can exist within an organization and should be explored. Participants should talk about what they see and why they scored the organization the way they did. Each perspective helps to better understand the organization's strengths and its weaknesses. Additionally, the group should consider both the individual expression of APEST at different campuses, or sub-group level (such as different ministries or services), as well as the expression of APEST throughout the entire organization. There is a list of helpful questions at the end of this appendix to help reflect on the test results and subsequently craft an action plan.

3. Organizational Profile Comparison—Capacity vs. Execution

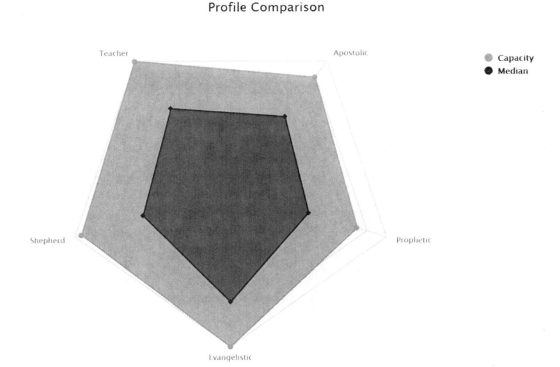

Figure A.7 Sample Profile Comparison Chart for Church A

The third results graph is the organizational profile comparison. This chart compares the combined **capacity** of the leadership team with the **demonstrable** functions of the organization. The total capacity of the leadership team (the aggregate capacity depicted in the *Organizational Leadership Profile*) is visualized as one solid area. The actual execution of APEST functions by the church is shown as a different solid color. (This is derived from the aggregated scores of how each individual on the leadership team assessed the organization.) There may not be a consensus regarding how the organization is functioning; different opinions in this assessment can lead to vital and informative conversations.

The purpose of the capacity comparison chart is, as it states, to compare the **capacity** inherent in the leadership team with the **execution** of those capacities within the organization. It is this relationship between capacity and execution that is most illuminating and key to the discussion of actionable next-steps.

There are three different possible results for this graph:

1. Leadership capacity is **greater** than church function

It is common for the leadership capacity to be greater than church functions, often because the abilities that lie within the leadership team take time to translate out into and across the organization, and also because the organization almost always lags behind leadership vision. This gap can also indicate how effective a church is at discipleship. Effective discipleship will involve leaders intentionally training and discipling others in the APEST functions so that they may understand and, in turn, train others.[31]

2. Leadership capacity is **the same as** church function

This means you are working to capacity in that area. Everything you have is moving from the leadership team and is being dispersed throughout the organization. The action steps for this result will clearly differ from those where there is a gap between the leadership capacity and the church function. In some churches, there is no gap between leadership and organizational function because the leaders have risen to their own level of competence.[32] It means that in order for the organization to grow and look more like Jesus, the leaders need to grow so that there is greater capacity within the whole organization. If leadership competencies are not higher than the organization's behaviors and both are low, the test will show the specific areas of development that can help correct that.

3. Church function is **greater** than leadership capacity

This means the life and activity of the church or organization is greater than the leadership capacity. The church function being greater could be caused by a God-given opportunity that the Body has stretched into that the leaders have not yet caught up with or engaged with (so leadership capacity needs to increase in its learning and skillset to keep up with, and steward, what God is doing). It could also mean that some members at the edge of the church are operating outside of connection and accountability with leadership.

The leadership capacity being lower could also be due to a leadership transition where the team has lost significant leadership capacity and is looking to recruit or train up more junior leaders from within (so there is a temporary competency gap in the leadership capacity as it relates to the church function). It could also be a wake-up call for the current leadership team of their need to grow in capacity and to seek training and investment.

These three possible results can all occur on the same graph, across the five functions. For example, in the shepherding function, the leadership capacity might be greater than the church function. This means that people need to be discipled in shepherding, and the organization needs to look at what aspects of shepherding people understand, but are failing to live out. If in the prophetic, for example, the leadership capacity is the same as the church function, then you might want to prioritize other areas, whilst ensuring that momentum isn't lost in the prophetic. And finally, as an example for the third possible result, in the apostolic, the church function might be greater than the leadership capacity, resulting in numerous pioneering activities, some of which may not be accountable, supported or sustainable because the leadership capacity does not match the church activity.

Each of these results will lead to different actionable steps—it is the relationship between the two capacities that is the most important and informative. There is a difference between the *capacity* of APEST in an organization that is held in the understanding of its leaders, and the *expression* of APEST functions through the organization. It is vital to discern this difference and to act upon it. Assessment of both is needed in order to specifically identify the areas of growth for an organization and to create correlating action plans.

Individual Domain Score Results in Depth

The chart below is a sample of individual scores. These scores are very different from an individual's APEST profile score[33] and should not be used as a substitute for an individual's profile. In fact, the individual results from this assessment are often different in some important ways from an individual's APEST profile. This does not mean that one test is correct and accurate and one is not. Rather, one is more a measurement of *calling* and innate gifting and the other is a measurement of *conceptual understanding*. The results cannot be directly correlated with one another. However, the comparison of the two will yield interesting insights. It is best to take both assessments because more can be understood about each individual when viewed in collaboration with an individual's APEST profile results.

Individual Domain Scores

		Alicia Johnson	Bob Henderson	Jessie Cruickshank	Peter Rawlins	Robert Cruickshank
Teacher	Teaching organizational function of creating a culture of learning	3.0	7.0	4.0	3.0	8.0
	Teaching organizational function of practical training (discipling)	4.5	1.5	4.0	7.0	2.5
	Teaching organizational function of creating a culture of accuracy and insight on theology and related disciplines	3.0	4.5	3.0	3.5	3.0
Evangelistic	Evangelistic organizational function of communication and storytelling	1.0	1.5	8.0	3.0	7.0
	Evangelistic organizational function of recruitment to the cause/ recruitment capacities	0.5	3.5	4.0	4.0	4.0
	Evangelistic organizational function of being pragmatic within the cultural context	0.5	2.0	3.5	2.0	2.0
Apostolic	Apostolic function of trans-local influence and networking	8.0	2.5	2.0	3.0	2.5
	Apostolic function of guardian of the DNA (core ideas, concepts and codes)	2.0	4.0	1.5	3.0	5.0
	Apostolic function of missional church planting	6.0	3.0	0.5	3.0	1.5
Prophetic	Prophetic organizational function of guardian of the covenant (our relationship with God, our agreement with God)	7.0	2.0	3.5	8.0	1.5
	Prophetic organizational function of the horizontal prophetic	2.5	1.0	3.0	3.0	3.5
	Prophetic organizational function of the vertical prophetic	5.5	3.5	6.0	5.5	3.5
Shepherd	Shepherding organizational function of protection of community and human relationships	3.0	2.0	3.0	1.5	3.0
	Shepherding organization functioning as the reconciled and redeemed Family of God, community development	3.5	3.0	3.0	6.0	2.0
	Shepherding organizational function of nurture and soul healing	3.0	2.0	1.0	3.0	1.5

Figure A.8 Sample Individual Domain Score Chart

When considering individual results from The Systems Analysis, especially in contrast to a person's APEST profile results, several things are worth noting:

Overdevelopment

Sometimes, individuals score higher in an area on the 5Q Systems Analysis than they are ranked on their individual APEST profile. Remember that an individual APEST profile helps a person discern what they are **passionate** about, how they see the world, and what their giftedness is. The Systems Analysis test helps measure what a person **understands** about the specific functions of APEST.

Understanding is not the same as passion. I may *know* a lot about computers, but that does not mean I have a *passion* or a gift for working with them. In fact, I may find that using my understanding about computers is quite exhausting and emotionally draining. At the same time, I may have a passion for building things out of wood. And even though I may not technically know much about it, I am naturally gifted at it and find it highly enjoyable. It is the same dynamic between the personal APEST profile and the analysis of current understanding.

As in my example with computer skills, people can be overdeveloped in an area beyond their passion and giftedness. This may occur because a particular ministry situation necessitates it. For example, one assisting minister scored high on shepherd on the 5Q assessment, but it was one of the lowest capacity on her individual APEST Profile. She had previously served under a senior pastor who was highly evangelistic but low in shepherding. This dynamic caused her to serve more in the shepherding capacities than she was naturally passionate or naturally gifted. It had been a frustrating and challenging season for her, and her main gifting—teaching—had not been utilized at all.

It's often said that leaders should "staff to their weakness," seeking people to help them in complementary ways. But a good leader also seeks to deploy and develop people in their areas of *strengths* and *passions*, rather than just their capabilities.

It is not inherently a bad thing to be overdeveloped in an area[34]—God has purpose in every season. Indeed, a leader who is overdeveloped in an area is likely to be a more effective leader when the season changes and they have opportunity to develop their strengths and move in their passions.

Underdevelopment

Many who take the assessment discover they are underdeveloped in the area in which they score highest on the individual APEST profile assessment.[35] There are two potential reasons for this.

Firstly, developing our own strengths is not as common as we think. We are often more focused on our weaknesses, working to fix what is broken, shore up what is weak, and learn the answers to questions missed. This means that our strengths are taken for granted, and we can find ourselves coasting on natural talent rather than learning how to improve the things we are already good at.

Secondly, we are often blind to our strengths. Our top area on the individual APEST profile is usually our underlying paradigm of the world. A fish isn't even aware of the water around it—it knows no other way of existing. Likewise, unexamined paradigms can be the lenses through which we see the world, but they are also lenses we never take off to consider how they might be developed or applied to another context. We don't become a student of our gifts, learning how to grow and improve, or consider what needs to be tweaked or adapted for a different context. Having an assumed paradigm can cause a person to be underdeveloped in their passions or stronger innate APEST capacities. We continue to operate in the intuition we have, but don't seek to intentionally grow in the area of our natural competency. As a result, we are not consciously aware enough to be truly mature or to teach others how we think and see the world; we haven't examined or reflected sufficiently on our gifting to be able to train and equip others in it.

Individual Expression of the APEST Capacities vs *Organizational* Expression of the APEST Capacities

There is a difference between the capacities functioning in an individual and functioning in an organization,[36] and the assessment highlights the difference in that understanding. This means that while someone may know what a healthy apostle (and an unhealthy one) looks like, their limited experience or limited exposure to the apostolic functions operating in an organization may cause that person to score lower on the assessment. So, the 5Q test results can highlight the difference between an individual's awareness of one of the APEST functions, and the expression of that same function within an organization.

Applying Insights from the Assessment Results

Organizations often reflect the strengths of their key leader because the key leader sets the priorities, determines the metrics, and to a large degree shapes the culture of the organization. For the same reasons, it is also common that organizations will reflect the weakness of their leaders as well.

The same correspondence is true for Christian groups or organizations as well. The founder sets the template. The whole "seeker-sensitive" movement of the late twentieth century was led by exemplary evangelists; the movement that has come out of Bethel Church in Redding, California, in the early twenty-first century is led by model prophets; John Piper is a teacher, and his church and organization are built to suit. And so on: The general rule is "as the leader so the people."

Leadership teams can often be similarly minded; people naturally gravitate towards those who think like themselves. If fivefold diversity isn't embraced in the core team, this can easily lead to communication issues and to marginalization of dissenting voices and ideas.

Character, motivations, attitudes, and management issues aside, working with people who operate from a different paradigm is challenging. We find it challenging to listen to, work with, and empower those who are different from ourselves. That is human nature. We believe that valuing and seeking a full APEST expression will bear more fruit and maturity than any particular church governance structure.

It is also essential to continually point ourselves back to Jesus for reorientation as both the standard and the example, as we lead others. Obviously not all of the disciples had the same paradigm as Jesus. But he discipled, mentored, empowered, and released them just the same.

Bridging the gap between the leadership team capacities and the organizational expression of APEST requires a number of things: discipleship, training, empowerment, release, along with effective systems and strategies. It is important to assess what the blockages or issues are that are hindering the church from living into its full APEST capacity. Careful reflection as a team can help identify what the appropriate next steps might be.

Crafting Your Action Plan

How you use your individual results in depth is up to you as a leadership team. There is no one-size-fits-all or silver bullet.

Some organizations have used them to help adjust job descriptions to reflect their passions more than just their competencies. Other have used them to identify areas of professional development, whether individually or corporately, by instituting internal training processes or engaging with outside help.

The important thing to remember is that the expressions of each of the APEST functions in an organization are many and varied—there is much to know and much to be explored. Prioritize, enjoy the journey, and trust that God—and not you—is the true author and finisher of your faith.

As you examine the assessment results and discuss them as a group, there are several methods to use that will help the graphs translate into actionable next steps.

1. Review the organizational leadership profile.

    i. Observe the strengths and weaknesses, symmetry and asymmetry.

    ii. Reflect on the results as individual team members.

iii. Discuss the results and your individual reflections as a team. Why do the leadership team members think this is? What personal insights might they bring to understand it better? How do they see things in the organization and what might they say is missing or confused?

iv. What does the group want to do about it? How serious does the group feel the situation is currently? Who, if anyone, might be a good fit and bring about balance to the leadership team? What, if any, disciplines or training could be engaged with to grow in this area of weakness or deficit?

2. Review the organizational functions profile and the comparison chart.

i. Observe the strengths and weaknesses, symmetry and asymmetry.

ii. Reflect on the results as individual team members.

iii. Discuss the results and your individual reflections as a team. Based on the scores each person gave the organization individually, where does the group agree on the organizational functions profile? Where does the group disagree? Why might that be the case?

iv. As a team, what do you agree are the organization's strengths and weaknesses? Do these mirror the senior leader? Do they mirror those on the leadership team?

v. Where is the capacity of the leadership group higher than the organization? What can be done to raise the expression of APEST across the organization?

vi. What is the weakest point in the profiles? How might you seek to remedy them?

vii. Where is the capacity of the leadership group the same as the organization? What could be done to increase the capacity of the leadership group to create space for a greater organizational expression? Do leaders need to undergo further development and training? If so, what?

viii. Where is the organizational expression greater than the leadership group's capacity? Is that due to a particular person or group's influence who are not on the current leadership team? If so, what does the group think about that? If not, what leading is the organization following that gives it capacity beyond its understanding, and how can the individuals on the leadership team increase in their understanding in that area? How can they learn more so that they can be more intentional and equip others to be more intentional?

3. Review individual results in depth.

    i. What over/under development does it demonstrate? Would each team member agree with the results of their own individual assessment? Would other team members affirm or disagree with the results of each individual assessment?

    ii. Do any job descriptions need to be reworked?

    iii. What professional development would be a priority individually?

    iv. Are there any places as a team or organization where there is the need for professional development (either an internal training process or external investment or input)?

4. Look at group processes and team dynamics.

    i. In the debrief of the results, try to remember the whole organism, and not just focus on the individual organs. Think about the connections—

- between the leadership team and other teams within the organization

- between each of the team members themselves

- between the team members and the team leader

- between the leadership team and others members of the organization.

And finally, think about how things are communicated and structured within the organization.

5. Diagnose and strategize together.

    i. Throughout the course of analyzing the results, debrief each other. Try to ask probing questions that look at the situation through different lenses and invite difference perspectives. This will help the group more accurately diagnose the issue. Use one or more of the APEST exercises in chapter five to develop competence in fivefold thinking and acting.

    ii. Try to separate the anecdotal answers (one person's experience or point of view) from the systematic evidence (for example, five out of seven small groups are operating in a certain way). The fact that a situation is anecdotal does not mean it is invalid. It just means that it needs to be addressed with a different strategy, such as a personal conversation. The scale of a strategy or remedy should match the scale of an issue.

iii. As a group, discuss strategies to address what you see currently and where you would like to get to (potentially using tools and tactics in chapter five). Create a final set of goals and actionable next steps.

As well as using these actionable next steps, please also refer back to the tools and tactics in chapter five, as well as the response you have noted in the 'Stop' boxes throughout this book, to help you move your team and your organization toward the next step in becoming a healthy, balanced expression of the fullness of Christ.

Notes

1   Hirsch, *5Q: Reactivating the Original Intelligence and Capacity of the Body of Christ* (Atlanta:100m Publications, 2017) available to buy at www.5qcentral.com/shop/ ; Hirsch & Catchim, *The Permanent Revolution* (San Francisco: Jossey-Bass, 2012).

2   APEST summary sheet designed by Kevin Miller, Community Pastor at Ecclesia Hollywood (www.churchinhollywood.com).

3   Institute for Health and Human Potential, "What is Emotional Intelligence?", www.ihhp.com/meaning-of-emotional-intelligence.

4   Gk. *edothe*, the aorist indicative form of *didomi*.

5   "καταρτίζω" *katartizō*, "to make, prepare, restore, establish, mend, repair, make whole or perfect, of setting bones, mending nets." C. Spicq and J. D. Ernest, *Theological Lexicon of the New Testament,* vol. 2 (Peabody, MA: Hendrickson, 1994), 271. Strong's Concordance says "2677 *katartismós* (a masculine noun), exact adjustment which describes how (enables) the individual parts to work together in correct order (used only in Eph 4:12) . . . complete furnishing, perfecting." See J. Strong, *A Concise Dictionary of the Words in the Greek Testament and the Hebrew Bible,* vol. 1 (Bellingham, WA: Logos Bible Software, 2009), 40.

6   "Failure to thrive syndrome" was first documented in Romanian orphanages in the late twentieth century. In it children were fed and clothed, and basic nutritional needs were met, but love and affection was not provided. These children failed to learn to speak, their growth was stunted to

less than four feet tall, and many died in their teenage years. We are social-emotional beings, and community is vital to all aspects of being human.

7   For a more thorough theological and cultural exploration of 5Q, we highly recommend reading the associated book 5Q: *Reactivating the Original Intelligence and Capacity of the Body of Christ (Atlanta:100m Publications, 2017).*

8   Because APEST is not exclusive to the first-century Christian church, it becomes impossible for it to have ever ceased based on the canonization of any text.

9   Just to be sure of what we are referring to here, when we use the language of domains, we are simply following theological tradition of referring to those extra-ecclesial dimensions of life that form the structures of society. In fact these too are part of the orders of creation that are disciplined, sanctified and redeemed by the Kingdom work of Jesus. We need to reiterate that while we believe that the Kingdom of God does call us to relate to, and work redemptively, in and among all the various domains of society, we do not personally adhere to the theocratic domination theology of the so-called New Apostolic Reformation along with the associated Seven Mountains movement. They rightly use the language of APEST, but in our opinion they generally have a hierarchical notion of leadership that runs clean contrary to the model that Jesus set for us to follow—that of the servant leader (Matthew 20:25-27; Philippians 2:1-11). Don't let the similarities of the language—which ironically is also used in Reformed theology—obscure the importance of the topic for the broader missional conversation of which we are very much a part. See a review of this movement by our friend and researcher Brad Sargent "Examining 'The Seven Mountains' Movement" 2009, www.bit.ly/1HjQrTl .

10 While we believe Paul is talking about the ministry of all believers (Ephesians 4:7: "to each one of us") leadership is at least implied in Paul's articulation of ministry.

11 Alan Hirsch and Michael Frost, *The Shaping of Things to Come: Innovation and Mission for the 21st-Century Church*, 2nd ed. (Grand Rapids, MI: Baker, 2013), 215. The first edition came out in 2003.

12 This is obvious when one thinks about how marketing and movie-making programs help mature evangelistic capacities. Business schools and most organizational development programs help mature apostolic capacities. Art schools, music programs, literature, political science, and some non-profit training can mature some prophetic capacities. Of course there is higher education for teaching in all domains. There are nursing and social work programs for shepherding capacities, although this domain might be the most underdeveloped in terms of secular programs that help mature the capacities.

13 By this we mean to remind people that the *ecclesia* is not a building but a living organism. We are not all called to go to a church building as a demonstration of our participation in the Kingdom of God. Rather we are called to bring the Kingdom and *be* the *ecclesia* in all aspects of society. We are the yeast in the dough, not people in a building.

14 This means the church can be relevant for more than just understanding Scripture – it can be relevant for understanding life and for equipping people in their callings, no matter what their vocation is. Seeing this as the purpose of the church is radically different from the one it has become, yet it is more in line with its original intent. And, we would argue, it increases the church's relevance in society.

15 The scope and purpose of this book prevents us from providing a detailed account of how Jesus is the quintessential expression of APEST. A more comprehensive account can be found in Hirsch, *5Q: Reactivating the Original Intelligence and Capacity of the Body of Christ (Atlanta:100m Publications, 2017.)* Also see Neil Cole, *Primal Fire* (Carol Stream, IL: Tyndale Momentum, 2014).

16 And if this seems novel to us, I believe this is largely because the language around some of these fivefold giftings (especially that around the apostolic) has become censured and has been politicized. I would argue that the fivefold patterning exemplified by Jesus actually expands our understanding of Christology in ways that get us beyond the somewhat reductionist traditional, tri-perspectival approach.

17 See J. A. Phillips, *The Form of Christ in the World: A Study of Bonhoeffer's Theology* (New York: Collins, 1967).

18 Some in the Calvinist tradition add church discipline as one of the marks.

19 We apologize for the biting tone here, but we are always flabbergasted at how ridiculously reductionist and short-sighted these really are. Honestly, of all the doctrines handed down to us through our traditions, we can think of few more that are so institutional, clerical, obtuse, and useless than the Protestant definitions of church.

20 Look at John 13:1–17, 34, 8:31; Mark 12:28–31; Matthew 28:16–20, etc. These are expected to be visible signs of Jesus' presence. And given the reduction of Jesus' church to the receiving of sacraments and the hearing of preaching, the marks are not only uninspiring, they bolster the authority of the religion institution. There is no explicit mention of God, nor even an implied recognition of the preeminence of Jesus in his church! But, how can we possibly define the church without any reference to the primacy of Jesus Christ? As our friend Neil Cole says, "If you can define

church without Jesus then you can do church without Jesus." It is a point well worth pondering.

21 Perhaps another example of a category error is to equate preaching (usually associated with the pulpit) with the prophetic function. It might well be that preaching can be prophetic, but it can also be evangelistic, or used to teach the community. Preaching is just a medium, APEST is the message. Be clear with definitions and distinctions upfront.

22 See Mike Breen with Paddy Mallon, *Knowing Your Role in Life* (3DM Publishing, 2006) and Mike Breen and Steve Cockram, *Building a Discipling Culture,* 2nd ed. (3DM Publishing, 2014), chap. 10. This description is taken largely from Alan Hirsch and Tim Catchim, *The Permanent Revolution Playbook*, which itself is a fantastic group learning tool.

23 APEST summary sheet designed by Kevin Miller, Community Pastor at Ecclesia Hollywood (www.churchinhollywood.com).

24 Names have been changed.

25 Visit www.5qcentral.com/training/ for more information on further training options.

26 J Schenck (*Teaching and the adolescent brain: An educator's guide* (New York: W. W. Norton, 2011).

27 This is very different from a bell curve. Learning should not look like a bell curve because that means at the end, nothing has changed.

28 It is the nature of authentic assessments to be both accurate and precise. This makes them inherently actionable. They are not blunt instruments that apply broad generalizations. They provide good information upon which reasonable actions can be determined.

29 We also recommend JR Woodward, *Creating a Missional Culture: Equipping the Church for the Sake of the World* (Downers Grove, IL: IVP, 2012), Neil Cole, *Primal Fire: Reigniting the Church with the Five Gifts of Jesus* (Carol Stream, IL: Tyndale Momentum, 2014).

30 For more information visit www.5qcentral.com/training/ .

31 Many churches feel under-resourced and ill-equipped to know *how* to train others and so the 5Q Collective has developed resources to help intentionally train others in the APEST capacities. For more information visit www.5qcentral.com/training/ .

32 This is called the Peter Principle in organizational theory. The idea is that in a bureaucracy everyone in an organization keeps on getting promoted until they reach their level of incompetence, at which point they stop being promoted. So, given enough time and enough promotion

levels, *every* position in a firm will be occupied by someone who can't do the job. This is often true in bureaucracies and, sadly it has to be said, in many tired old mainline churches. For an explanation of the Peter Principle, see for instance Rob Asghar, "Incompetence Rains, Er, Reigns: What The Peter Principle Means Today" Forbes, www.goo.gl/hG6qMm .

33 You can take the personal profile assessment at www.5qcentral.com/tests .

34 As long, as it's not vastly out of pace with the development of other areas.

35 Unfortunately, many of those I have worked with who demonstrated to be underdeveloped in their strongest individual APEST capacity and overdeveloped in a low one have been women. I can only speculate at the myriad of reasons this may be so, from being happy to simply have a job in ministry when so many are not allowed, to a paradigm of being a "complementary" personality and thus not pressing for release in one's passions. Regardless, of the women I assessed, a full half of them were in the wrong position for their God-given gift mix. I would not consider such to be good stewardship of them by leadership.

36 Alan Hirsch, *5Q* (2017) explores this difference and its significance in depth.

CPSIA information can be obtained
at www.ICGtesting.com
Printed in the USA
LVOW09s0219140318
569803LV00015B/541/P